In the Eye of the Hawk

Reflections along the Potomac

Martin Ogle

ILLUSTRATIONS BY NICKY STAUNTON

D0883689

To Cyrus and Linnea

And in memory of Lynn Margulis

TABLE OF CONTENTS

CONTENTS

FOREWORD

By Lynn Margulis,
Distinguished University Professor
Department of Geosciences, University of Massachusetts

This is a book of love, and like love itself, it cannot be rushed. The object of love and respect, here, is Earth herself, as experienced through one small place on our blue-green planet. This place is a 100-acre forest of calm as well as adventure that the author knows the way a young lover knows his beloved's body. He sees and experiences it as a tapestry of opposites and harmonies: characteristic stillness subject to the outburst of an avian dust bath, nestled in the heights above the peaceful and stately Potomac River, surrounded by the madding crowd of Washington DC. Sometimes it is gray and at other times the land explodes in a riotous show of spring flowers or yellow-orange leaves.

A sanctuary for urban wildlife, this special place is, nonetheless, interrupted hundreds of times a day by jet noise and circumnavigated by the incessant hurry of motor vehicles. Ogle's narrative is a reminder that human beings are a part of this world. This parkland within a city, with 500-million years of geological history and more than ten thousand years of human habitation, has a spokesman who speaks of life for all of us.

This book bears a special message to our increasingly urban world, especially inhabitants of the "megalopolis" stretching from the Connecticut coast through New York City, Philadelphia, Baltimore and

Washington, D.C. and ending, more or less at the author's home base, Arlington, Virginia. The story blends what came long before humans with vignettes of people who have been part of the land and offers an alternative vision to urban hubris. Ogle's strong voice is not angry, however, but melodious. His worldview, enlightened by both science and the wisdom of our elders, is grounded in a place.

The book is unabashedly centered; sensing and sensed by the island of forest. The eyes of white-tailed deer sharply focus on the narrator, while he, in turn, watches an osprey hovering above green and yellow patches of lichen. Although replete with scientific information and incidental human interest, Ogle's theme is always clear and his prose accessible. As Naturalist of Potomac Overlook Regional Park, he keenly observes many different animals - including people – but he never argues from authority. Rather he represents only Nature, good sense and himself. His cheerful humility in the face of Nature's awesome power delights me. He gently nudges us to realize that we are and always have been intertwined with Nature's cycles. His story is a celebration of life itself and the living of a centrally grounded life.

With not a preachy word nor supercilious prejudice, this book is, in effect, a deeply religious history of a current landscape. The author captures details of his geological past, as when the Potomac flowed furiously over what is now high, dry land. He recounts human inhabitants building wigwams and long houses and follows their yearly cycles of planting, harvesting and migrations. And, while doing so, Ogle's quaint use of uppercase nouns keeps us mindful of inherent harmonies between Humans and Nature as a whole that are so obscured by the false dichotomization intrinsic in phrases like "Human versus Nature" or "Human *or* animal." We have here a sweet call to attentiveness that brings joy: the concentration of the new mother to glistening young eyes or the hunter's apprentice to the sharpened blade. To live, and how to live is the author's message. Ogle's understated erudition is an aspect of his originality. We learn from his first-hand observations: the fallen trees form horizontal Gaian terraces as they collect soil that serves their seedlings well; ancient beer bottles, ceramic shards and oyster shells show through a muddy bank to reveal glimpses into the lives of Italian-American quarry workers in the early 1900's.

Most remarkably, the book you now hold in your hand is baldly honest. Its naked authenticity makes the author's narrative relevant to our megapolitan malaise. Ogle shares with us what "he knows", really knows first-hand, and on this firm foundation invites and tests observations and thoughts of others. Ogle weaves in stories from his young life in Korea, Stone Mountain (Georgia), and Wisconsin, and, later, from Northern California and other places. But he always spirals back to his present and long-time home, and he leaves us with a vision of what life might be like in this place at some time in the future.. What a glorious way to spend a weekend or a spring vacation: listen enthralled as Ogle's tale takes you beyond the pages and brings you into the calm and glory of Nature who sustains and nurtures us.

INTRODUCTION

In the early years of the 21st century, there has been a surge of interest in how people relate to Earth. The discovery – and rediscovery – of simpler and "down to Earth" ways of living have contributed to this interest. So have looming energy and food crises, prospects of global warming and the loss of biodiversity. Along with these discoveries and concerns has come another realization: people of all ages are increasingly mired in sedentary, overly structured, indoor lifestyles that are quite unhealthy and do not permit an understanding of Earth and how we fit in with its living systems. A nationwide movement has arisen to connect kids, in particular, directly with the world around them – to get them playing outside, away from TV and computer screens and exploring their surroundings in unstructured ways.

This is a noble endeavor for the statistics are clear and alarming: growing rates of obesity and diabetes in children and adults; vastly reduced "roaming areas" where kids are allowed to explore and spend time; and a populace unfamiliar with where food, energy and other resources of daily life come from. Getting kids outdoors is only part of the story, however. Greater mobility, increasing urbanization and other forces that arose after World War II weakened a "sense of place" for many Americans. Real and perceived safety concerns and a frenetic over-structuring of children's lives during the past couple decades have further widened the schism between people and the lands in which we live. Drawn to our computers, I-phones and other video screens, large and small, we shut ourselves indoors, and experience the world indirectly and at a faster pace.

In 2008, my wife, Lisa, and I welcomed two marvelous, new lives into this world – our twins, Cyrus and Linnea. Their growth, discovery and antics have delighted us and we watch their developing personalities with love and fascination. And, our sense of responsibility for the future has been heightened as well. To a greater extent than ever before, I am compelled to address the challenges of our times and to provide my children with the tools they will need to do so themselves. I have completed the writing of this book as part of that charge, filling it with many of the stories and insights that they will hear and experience as they grow up. When they are old enough, perhaps they will read the book themselves and gain a greater understanding of all those stories and things that Dad shared with them.

While Cyrus and Linnea are young, my wife and I are working to provide them with freedom and time to explore and learn – at a slow pace and largely in the outdoors. We want to spare them many of the myriad distractions of our overscheduled and materially-preoccupied world and, at the same time, keep them attuned to the ideas, trends and skills of society at large. I'd like my children to be able to "ground themselves" in the place or places they live; to learn and internalize the stories, histories and perspectives that make up the character of a place. I want them to be able to see beyond the superficial, often opaque, patina of modern society that so often separates us from real appreciation and understanding of how our lives are a seamless continuum with all of Life. I want them to learn skills of self-reliance *and* community-reliance; self confidence and self respect. I hope they can acquire the temperament and skills that allow them to provide at least some of the food, shelter, goods and services they need from the place they live, and perhaps *almost everything* they need in cooperation with people they know and trust. I want my children to learn how to forge relationships with their place: first – but then always – through fun and exploration, then through reason, experimentation and a sense of responsibility as they grow older.

In keeping with the hopes and dreams for my children, this book is a series of perspectives about a place in which seemingly disparate aspects of life find meaning in the context of the relationship between people and land. A reasonably thorough accounting of local geology is juxtaposed with a whimsical tale about a squirrel; attention to the practicalities of feeding and keeping ourselves warm are followed by a more esoteric perspective on how we view time; stories from the past and other places are interspersed with descriptions of the here and now; a tale of love lost and the lessons it taught me are a part of the mix.

The book reflects my *own* sense of place which morphed, at some point in my thirties, beyond a simple *appreciation* of the area in which I live into a feeling of being woven into its very fabric. As I became aware of this transition, I was compelled to write about it, but found that the connections I wished to convey did not lend themselves to a chronological accounting. Instead, my thoughts seemed to gather around a circular sense of time – itself, one of the insights from my place. These essays and stories might be thought of as memories or dreams that come to mind as I tell stories with friends, try to draw practical guidance from the living land or relive the days, seasons and other cycles of this living land. Beyond any insights the individual vignettes might offer, however, they derive from and point to something of much greater significance – the interwoven tapestry of Life.

The title of the book, "In the Eye of the Hawk," reflects a memory from my own childhood and a number of subsequent experiences. It also alludes, symbolically, to positive visions of the future. I'd like for Cyrus and Linnea to envision and help create the world they want; not to feel stuck in a life created by mistakes of the past. I invite you, the reader, to peer through the same lens and perspectives that will color my children's discovery of their place and the creation of their future.

When you arrive at the last essay, *A Vision*, compare and contrast your own vision of a future with mine. Mull it over. Share your thoughts with friends and kids. Write your own vision.

A short autobiographical sketch will lend further context to this book, for the frequent moves of my early life certainly contributed to my desire for being more centered in place as an adult. I was born and raised much of my younger years in South Korea, the son of Methodist Missionaries. My father went to Korea just after the Korean War, finding a tattered landscape, power struggles, and an energetic and cheerful people. A big part of his work was labor relations; trying to better the awful working conditions of employees in steel mills, textile mills and coal mines. When he returned to the U.S. in the late 1950s, he met and married my mother, and within a short time, they returned to Korea. I still marvel at my parents' adventurous spirits, but especially my Mother's daring. As a 23-year-old newlywed, she braved the month-long trip across the Pacific aboard a freighter to a strange and wonderful place, without knowing much of its language or customs. My three sisters and I were all born in Korea, and being among just a few foreign families in the city of Inchon, stood out as blond-haired oddities in a sea of shiny black. I attended a few years of Korean school, becoming fluent in the language and fitting in as best I could, which was, at best, self-consciously. I have long since forgotten a great deal of the Korean language, but constantly discover ways in which the language and culture are etched in my mind and behavior.

My family returned three times to the United States; we lived in Madison, Wisconsin on two of those occasions, and moved to Decatur, Georgia during my high school years. Our final trip back to the U.S. was the result of my father being expelled from Korea by the military dictatorship there. He had brought to light the predicament of eight men from the countryside being accused as communist sympathizers. The Korean CIA seized him and demanded that he sign papers promising he would no longer meddle in South Korean affairs. He refused. To preserve their grip on power, the South Korean government maintained that North Korea was always on the verge of attack, and seemed to find new threats popping up everywhere. Later, while my sisters and I coped with culture shock in Georgia, the eight men were put to death in Korea. As you might expect, this event (and those that led up to it) had a profound impact on my young mind. It was numbing to consider the injustice and cruelty of the system that resulted in the torture and wrongful death of fellow humans. Amazingly, a couple decades later, the men were officially cleared of all crimes by a later Korean administration. Surely, if sensibilities and conditions could change that much in just 20 years, these and other atrocities need not have happened at all. These horrific events and ensuing changes informed my impressionable teenage mind.

Our family's frequent moves were both exciting and difficult for me – new places brought new experiences and friends, but added to my self-consciousness. I never felt quite at home at Shamrock High School in Decatur, and for the subsequent seven years, I was a nomad - college in Georgia, Colorado and Virginia, and work in Colorado, Idaho and Maryland. I reveled in the beauty and discovery of these places, but struggled with their inconsistencies and the need to constantly forge new relationships. My schooling was in wildlife biology and my jobs included leading youth backpacking trips, measuring radio-nuclides in wildlife at a nuclear testing facility and trapping, and banding and following the movements of Bald Eagles on Chesapeake Bay. The wandering stopped when, in 1985, I settled down in Arlington, Virginia and became a park manager and naturalist – a career that has continued for two and a half decades.

When I began my work at Potomac Overlook Regional Park, I did not imagine that I would end up living in Arlington so long, but was immediately hungry to know everything about this new place; there was at least the potential that I might stay here longer than anywhere *else* I had lived. I walked and biked almost every street and trail in Arlington, read history and natural history books about the area and immersed myself in volunteer work with Arlingtonians for a Clean Environment, the Arlington/Alexandria Coalition for the Homeless, and the Arlington Heritage Alliance. I went often – and still go – to the river to fish, walk and swim (yes, the Potomac is swimmable). I reawakened gardening skills I had learned as a child and found ways to use the solar and wood energy that my place provided in my daily life.

The transition from a simple appreciation of this place to something deeper began in the early 1990s, after I had lived in Virginia about 5 years. In 1991, I had the opportunity to revisit Korea for the first time since our family left there in 1975, and thus reconnected with some of my cultural roots. Then, in 1992, I visited Sweden, where my mother's side of the family had come from. In Sweden, I glimpsed part of my genetic heritage, and also came to realize the cultural ubiquity of the circle and four directions motif that forms the structure of this book. The Maypole dances in Sweden, the Scandinavian and Buddhist swastika symbols, the design of the Korean flag, the stories and symbols of North American Indians . . . I was finding that many cultures around the world have shared a remarkably similar view of how Life works and how people fit in.

From this perspective, I began to draw together the seemingly disparate elements of my life within in the context of the place I was now living.

Thus, this story of place incorporates experiences and stories from many *other* places – near and far – as well. People, ideas and philosophies fly in like birds from far away and become enmeshed with the local. Outside influences constantly become part of this place. Diseases from foreign lands infiltrated decades or centuries ago, killing trees and people. Geologic processes millions of years past, or hundreds of miles removed, pre-determined the very location of the human community in which I live. Stories from my *own* past and those of other citizens of this land have become enmeshed with this community. The ideas and values that became part of me as I grew up in Korea have had an impact on the look and feel of *this* place, especially now that I have lived and worked here for decades. The park's gardens, landscapes, and activities, for example, are colored by the orient: veiled paths lend a sense of mystery and space; simple rituals in some of our programs convey complex meanings; the yin-yang symbol is sometimes used to convey the scientific principle of negative feedback. As you will see, my descriptions of this place and even what I choose to highlight in this book and daily work are influenced by Korean sensibilities. Thus, East meets and blends with West here on a continual basis. From this tiny slice of life, alone, it only stands to reason that our own human stories become part of the stories of any place on Earth

To reflect the lessons I have learned from my place, I have organized this book into four main chapters that reflect the symbolism of the four cardinal directions. Each chapter can be read separately or in any order, but I end with a vision of how life might be in this place at some time in the future.

I have also taken some liberties with words and language to help chip away at the mental barriers that prevent our understanding of our relationship to Nature. For example, the casual characterization of things Human-made (buildings, chemicals, nylon, and so on) as being "unnatural" creates a dichotomy in our minds between "Nature" on one hand and "Humanity" on the other. An alien, observing Life evolve from afar, however, would not see this dichotomy, instead seeing clearly that we Humans grew out of this Earth as surely as did beavers and spiders. We have emerged from this planet, and our products are no less natural than beaver lodges or spider webs.

I have also drawn attention to some words that have been de-capitalized (literally and in their emphasis and understanding) in modern society and *re*-capitalized them to remind us of their fundamental character and importance. These words include: Nature, Earth, Human Being, Universe, Life, the four directions (North, South, East and West), and the four seasons (Spring, Summer, Fall and Winter). If, as you read, this unfamiliar capitalization catches your eye, take that second to focus on how basic the word is to our understanding of Life; how much richness is missed when we speed past the word in its un-capitalized forms. Why, for instance, do we often find the word "earth" spelled with a lower case "e" when all of the other planets are capitalized? Why, when the four directions and four seasons have played central roles in all ancestral cultures in temperate climates, are they not capitalized like the names of the months?

It is healthy and wise for people to understand and feel comfortable with the grand, interwoven flow of Nature of which we are a part. There is joy and satisfaction in the rediscovery of the places we live. And, from these insights come visions for meaningful, prosperous lives. Let us explore . . .

"We shall not cease from exploration, and the end of all our exploring shall be to arrive where we started and know the place for the first time."
– T .S. Eliot

CHAPTER 1

The South

Knowing and nurturing our place

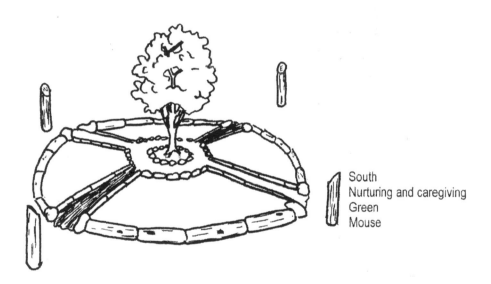

South
Nurturing and caregiving
Green
Mouse

W e step into the circle from the South to sense the grand cycles of Life and to come to know our place more deeply. By doing so, we develop our ability to nurture and care for our place, and, in turn, come to understand it even better. All of Life is a circle of which we are a part.

1

Here and Now

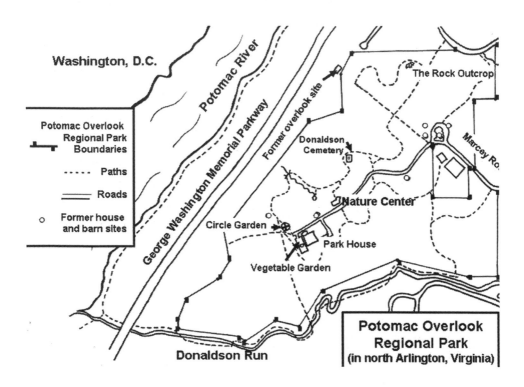

Nestled in a well-to-do neighborhood in Arlington, Virginia – within what was the original diamond-shaped boundary of the District of Columbia, and a long stone's throw from the Potomac River – are a hundred or so acres of woods. A couple small streams drain the rolling land and descend quickly to the river. Most of this urban woodland is called Potomac Overlook Regional Park and I have been the park's manager and naturalist for most of my adult life. My own story has become interwoven with that of this land, and my experiences gather in a orbit around this place like planets around a sun. As much as the tales that follow reflect this place, they also illuminate a much larger story that can reveal itself *any*where on Earth.

Imagine yourself flying into Washington, D.C.'s National Airport over the Potomac River, from the Northwest. If, a few minutes before landing, you peered out a window on the right side of the airplane, you might see a surprisingly large expanse of woods, and, if you looked closer, you might notice a curious, circular garden in the midst of the forest. If you were lucky enough to spot it at just the right moment, you would see that the garden was divided into four quadrants by two paths – one running North/South and the other running East/West – creating a cross. At the intersection of the two paths, in the center of the circle, is a tree. If you were to be curious enough to find that garden, you would find that the tree symbolized the center of the Universe and was referred to as the "Tree of Life." That forest is Potomac Overlook Regional Park and the circle on the ground is the park's Indian Circle Garden.

Each of the four directions of the circle garden has a symbolic color, animal and attribute. Many of these are surprisingly consistent through many cultures, and have been incorporated into the interpretation of the garden. South is the direction of Summer and its color is green. The animal of the South is the mouse, and the attribute is that of care-giving and nurturing. West is the direction of Fall and of the setting Sun. The color is black, the black bear is the symbolic animal, and the attribute is introspection. North, the direction of Winter, is symbolized by white, the swan and the attributes of strength and endurance. East is the direction of Spring and of the rising Sun. The color is yellow, the animal is the hawk or the eagle and the attribute is vision. (Of all of the symbolic animals used in the park's circle garden, the swan is the only one not commonly found in Native American stories.)

Although the circle garden is based on the medicine wheel of the Indians of North America (the specific idea for the garden came from a children's book *The Indian Way* by Gary McLain[1]), essentially the same symbol – a circle with a cross through it – is found all over the world. One encounters it in China's Temple of Heaven, Buddhist mandalas from Tibet, Irish mazes, British henges, and the Christian cross, which is often portrayed on the background of a circle. The ubiquity of this symbol may reflect a deep, organic truth about Humanity – that of our connection to place. Recent archaeological research suggests an intriguing distinction of *Homo sapiens* from other closely related apes, including other hominids of the past. In search of food we migrated out and back from a shifting center. This attachment to the place from which tribal members fan out has been called "home base foraging strategy" and hunter-gatherer peoples living today use it. Knowledge of the edible and useful plants and animals at a single base camp may have ensured our survival when other species of the Human genus, *Homo*, died out.

At Potomac Overlook, the Indian Circle Garden has been used for many years in a variety of programs and activities to underscore and explain concepts about local Human or Natural history, and especially relationships between the two. How does the Sun travel through the sky and how does this change with the seasons? How did people site and orient gardens and homes? How have equinoxes and solstices been significant in biological systems and Human cultures? The circle garden was constructed as a Boy Scout project and has been tended by hundreds of people since. Their individual efforts blend as one and make the garden a stronger focal point over time.

To inaugurate our first Indian history program incorporating the circle garden, we invited three Indian people, who were part of the development of the National Museum of the American Indian in Washington, D.C., to participate. After an indoor talk about local Native American history and culture, the group walked through the woods and arrived at the garden from the East. Just as we began discussion about the symbolic animal of the East, one of the participants pointed skywards and cried out "look!" There, soaring in circles about a hundred feet over our heads, was a Bald Eagle, its white head and tail unmistakable. To the three Native Americans – whose own tribes' stories paralleled others that had been told that day – the eagle's presence was a powerful omen. To many Native Americans, eagles and hawks symbolize vision – the ability to see into the future and to inspire people with images of how Life could be.

Our relationship with Nature, like Nature itself, is cyclical, and our ancestors realized this at a most fundamental level. Circle motifs and stories may be archetypal – evolutionarily hardwired into our individual and collective consciousness – and they are powerful lenses through which to view our relationship with Nature. Like a long-neglected treasure map, sitting dusty and rolled up on a shelf, these symbols and stories await our rediscovery and use.

Settling Into Place

The grand flow of life is sometimes experienced in a microcosm. Such was the case one trying day many years ago when I plopped myself, stiff and weary, on a park bench. Cares and worries weighed on me and troubled thoughts buzzed about my head like a swarm of whirligig beetles careening randomly on a pond. My mind was agitated and I was oblivious to my immediate surroundings. Suddenly, my self-imposed bubble was pierced by the snap of a branch and my senses were riveted on a large, living creature standing just a few yards away. It was a deer, chewing its food in the lazy side-to-side manner of a ruminant. A thin string of saliva hung from a hair on its chin. Brown eyes focused sharply on me and large ears twitched, but otherwise the creature did not appear overly concerned by my presence. She walked slowly past me and into a clearing just beyond the garden paths, calmly munching her evening meal.

As some time passed, I realized that there were several other deer in the woods behind the first. They progressed almost soundlessly through the underbrush, like a gathering of big-eared monks, solemn in their demeanor. My body began to relax as it followed my mind away from earlier abstractions and into the moment. Now, the richness of my surroundings – the deer, the smell of Spring soil, activity of the birds, the dappled, late afternoon sunlight – flooded my senses like an advancing tide. I was awakened.

I was also swept up in a different time scale than the one with which I had arrived, and my perceptions changed accordingly. When earlier worries did reenter my mind, they were less insistent. They seemed to blend with the scene before me – the dainty, yellow cast of spicebush blooms, a chunk of quartz resplendent with streaks of iron-red and tiny, new leaves of a box-elder trembling in the breeze. I steeped in the quiet pulse of Life. Later, when I reassessed my day, problems seemed less urgent, more solvable. I was refreshed. More profoundly, I had a brief, but intimate, perception of being bound to my place.

We have all had experiences similar to this in one form or another. Whether through a long walk, a meditation or a talk with a friend, we became centered. Problems and frustrations that previously seemed overwhelming were seen in a context that enabled us to understand and deal with them. Every so often, these reveries offer new insights or perspectives – like being reconnected to the world around us – or produce a sense of calm or satisfaction. We may involuntarily take and release a deep breathe.

The world often presents us, as individuals and as societies, with challenges and questions. How do we relate with other people and with the world around us? How do we find fulfilling work and relationships? How do we conduct our lives in healthy, meaningful ways and enable the same for our children and their future? What do we do in the face of vast wealth juxtaposed with dire poverty and the despoliation of living systems? How we understand and answer these questions – in word and deed – gives our lives form and character. These matters deserve a fresh perspective; demand our calm and grounded attention. In the rushed and disjointed society of 21st century America, however, we are increasingly separated from the grandeur, delight and stately pace of Nature all around us. Computer screens, TV and overly structured lives exert their pull on adults and children, alike, turning our collective thoughts inward. In our preoccupation, we become oblivious to our immediate surroundings and weighed down with cares and worries.

Can we burst from our self-imposed bubbles – collectively and individually – and allow the places we live to flood our senses and put our Human affairs in context? Becoming more aware of our place can help. A deep sense of place includes knowing our geographic space, our history, and the plants, animals and other life forms that live with us. It means coming to a heartfelt understanding that we are *interwoven* with that place and it with us. It means paying attention to Life around us – whether through sudden insight or long association. This is difficult in a day when we uproot and move from state to state or country to country without a second thought to the intricate systems we enter or leave. Difficult, but not impossible; difficult, but full of joy and discovery; difficult, but one of the greatest needs in our disconnected world.

We Humans are a *part* of Nature, not *apart* from it. We are not disconnected individuals occasionally plucking sustenance, meaning, or goods and services from otherwise separate surroundings. We are not detached from Life. Even as we consider these words, for example, the unconscious desire of our bodies for air prompts us to breathe – to carry on an exchange that links us to an impossibly long story extending to and beyond the very beginnings of Earth. Very late in this story, Human Beings grew *out* of Earth – as social beings of tribes, villages, and nations. We are inextricably tied to Earth's ancient Life system; our bodies, minds, emotions and even our stories are biological emanations of our living planet. Our history is a part of the land's story.

The idea that we arose *from* Life implies links. It ties individuals to families, families to Human society and all of these to Nature as a whole. These relationships are best understood within the context of the places we experience in everyday life. Conversely, if place is forgotten or obscured – when we are unaware of our relationships with Nature as a whole – other relationships may suffer. The calm, rooted disposition we wistfully refer to as "down to Earth" is supplanted by an unsettled feeling and we are distracted from what is around us. How do we return our attention to the land of which we are a part? Peoples who are *indigenous* to a place – whose culture literally grew out of a place like a tree arises from soil – often draw their connections to Nature with various forms of the circle and four directions symbol. So, let's continue to travel the circle.

River Rock

Atop a large rock jutting into the Potomac River, I sit quietly as a storm swirls around me. Amid a sphere of madness, I am nestled in a gently turning wrinkle in time. Human Beings hurtle over me at fantastic speeds in long tubes held aloft by wings of aluminum. Boxes of steel transport their Human contents North, East, South and West, along and across the river. Not far downstream, people even zoom through a tube *beneath* the river, back and forth, connecting with the rest of the storm of metropolitan Washington, D.C. All are moving fast, thinking fast. Fast, fast, fast.

I turn over and lie on my stomach atop the perch of ancient granite gneiss, and behold another rhythm. I see yellow-green lichens holding steadfastly to their nooks in the rock just above the waterline. How they shine in the Sun; not the glinting shine of mica crystals they bedeck, but a golden glow. They are so slow. The thought that they grow even slower than my toenail enters my head and amuses me. I ponder it. Slowly. The lichens occupy their rough little retreats like soldiers in a foxhole as the storm swirls around them as well.

Suddenly, with folded wings and screaming speed, an Osprey plummets into the river, overwhelming my erstwhile world of lichens and slowness. As the bird emerges from the water, ruffling its feathers and holding a prize of fish in its talons, a goldfinch roller-coasts by, flaunting its golden suit and black cap. On my ancient, lichen-encrusted rock, I am accompanied by Osprey, goldfinch, a flock of cormorants and a water snake as well. The tide has ebbed and the Sun is well across the sky. I have not seen one Human Being with whom to self-consciously make eye contact or exchange a nod or conversation. A Red-tail Hawk lands on a dead oak nearby. It utters no greeting or news of the day, but is aware of my presence and knows, in its own way, that we are bound by the circle.

I stare down into the eddy. It has captured a raft of pondweed and a damselfly in its vortex. With the September Sun beating gently on my back, I am content. As brown floodwaters gurgle by, I recall folded sheets of slushy ice that the river had crumpled up against this rock eight months earlier when the Sun shone low in the sky through bare trees.

Then, as now, there was no Human presence. The sycamores stood silent watch.

Presently, I sit back upright and, in my imagination, make my way to the riverbank and climb up to a promontory that affords a view of this very rock. From there, I behold the river and picture myself down below on the throne of gneiss, staring down into the eddy with a damselfly at its vortex. My fantasy carries me into space, looking down upon the whole scene – an eddy in time with me at its center. Like the damselfly, I am in the eye of a storm, and I revel in that awareness.

The sweet, subtle smell of decaying water plants wafts on the gentle breezes and brings me back to the moment. The smell of decline – of a world beginning to rest –comforts me as much as the vibrant sensations of May when the land shone like emeralds with fresh new leaves and the air smelled of moist Earth. The grand cycles of Life are not separate from the Human experience, but they do precede us; they are our foundation and nourishment. From the rock, I consider all of this and nod my head in agreement with the Universe.

Heat

On hot days, Life simultaneously slows down and speeds up. Venturing out on a stiflingly humid, 100-degree day for which the Washington D.C. area is famous, one feels like a sleepwalker, unable to muster the energy for anything more than a shuffle. Like blood from a cut, sweat beads up with the slightest exertion. Heat shimmers off any sunny surface, a furnace. Everything appears to move in slow motion. In the gathering breeze, the treetops roll in a slow wave. In the tiny world, however, things are different.

A whir! A barely perceptible touch on my arm. Before I could look down, there was another whir, and a shape darted out into the sunlight and then returned, again landing on my arm. I glanced down to assess my tiny guest, a handsome little butterfly of olive, black, and grayish-brown hues with a smattering of black eyespots and white blotches glimmered in the sunlight. Its antennae were boldly marked with tiny black and white horizontal stripes and white club-shaped tips. The insect was still for just a moment before it fluttered frantically off again only to return to the exact same spot, its proboscis extending to a bead of my sweat!

I suppose this dainty hackberry butterfly craved minerals in my perspiration! For almost a minute, the insect performed its sip-and-fly routine. Even as I turned to head down the path, the little sweat-monger followed me, performing rapid aerial exercises and alighting on me again and again. Then when I wiped the sweat off my arm with my shirt, the little pest landed right on my nose just long enough for me to go cross-eyed!

Since that occasion, I've experienced a salt-hungry hackberry butterfly two or three times and no other butterflies or moths have followed me so aggressively. I wonder if this species has a propensity for such behavior and, playfully, if I have the aroma of a hackberry tree. Whatever the case, this association allowed me to instantly recognize the relatively dull-colored little insect. I have fun with its scientific name, *Asterocampa celtis* and that of hackberry trees, *Celtis occidentalis*, on which the butterfly's caterpillars feed. And I ponder the different effects that extreme heat has on creatures great and small. Connections are felt and forged at multiple levels.

* * * * * *

One stifling late-August afternoon, I witnessed another flurry of activity in the world of the small. It was perhaps the hottest day of the decade – 102 or 103 heavy, moist degrees. I stood motionless and wilted in the garden clothed only in loose shorts. Suddenly into this oven appeared two small puffs of dust, whirls of movement. Two tiny birds flapped and fluttered about in a patch of dry, cooked soil. These handsome little birds with blue-gray backs, white fronts and long tails whirred and stirred, seemingly indifferent to the heat that muted my own existence. In the midst of this scorching, hot day, these Blue-gray Gnatcatchers were taking dust baths!

The gnatcatchers threw themselves into paroxysms of puffed up feathers and rolling ecstasy. They shook their bodies in waves like a dog shakes off water, leaning first one way and then the other. Hopping, swirling and dancing in the dust, the birds transcended their avian inability to form facial expressions; they seemed to grin with joy and contentment! I could almost share in their relief as they shook, rubbed off and asphyxiated all manner of parasites from their bodies.

The incongruity of the situation still fills me with wonder. In that heat, simply lifting my arm was an effort producing a tangible need to cool myself. And yet, these tiny, feathered creatures vibrated with wings a-blur! Why didn't they simply boil over in their enthusiasm? Like all birds, Blue-gray Gnatcatchers have extremely high body temperatures – over 100 degrees. To deal with the enormous metabolic heat produced by the powerful movements of flight, birds have developed a very efficient method of ridding their bodies of excess heat. By simultaneously inhaling and exhaling in a circular breathing pattern, they transfer large amounts of air and heat quickly. Like my old VW Beetle, theirs is an air-cooled engine! This circular breathing also ensures a continuous flush of oxygen necessary to fuel their fire-like metabolism.

In the even tinier world of plant chloroplasts, too, the pace is fast on a hot, sunny day. Photosynthesis speeds up, transferring the energy of sunlight to high energy molecules that are used by the plant to produce sugars. On hot summer days, we can practically *see* the furious growth of plants – especially that of the non-native bittersweet, porcelain-berry and the aptly named mile-a-minute vine. These Asian vines, seemingly freed from other limits to their growth in the new world, grow rampantly up and over shrubs and trees. The energy that green plants wrest from the Sun also indirectly powers the activity of the hackberry butterfly, the Blue-gray Gnatcatcher and most of the rest of us. The Sun is the ultimate energy source of my own life, this woodland, my family, my nation and the whole Human race. Energy fixed by plants trickles turns the cycles of Life like running water turns a waterwheel. As I touched my hot forehead, I was reminded that all of this energy captured by plants is converted back to heat and eventually escapes back to space, shimmering off of our living planet.

As I turned away from the avian antics to return to the coolness of my house, an airplane roared overhead. I sensed acutely the tremendous heat produced by its engines. A jet runs on the energy of fuel distilled from oil that, in turn, holds the energy captured from the Sun by algae millions of years ago. The energy stored in an immense bank account of fossil fuels offers temporary speed and huge amounts of heat.

A Surprise

Colonel McLaughlin walked his dog, Suzie, in the park almost every day. I'd often see them on the park road and would stop to chat. The

Colonel was an erect, trim man who kept his thinning gray hair in a very short buzz cut and almost always wore a pair of sunglasses with small, dark lenses. He was very polite and sincere in his mannerisms and I enjoyed his company. Suzie was a small, brown dachshund that stood barely 9 inches tall at the shoulder. Her pointed little tail would practically wag itself off her body when you said her name.

One lovely and bright sunny day, I saw the Colonel and Suzie at the end of the park road, just where it turns into a trail heading into the woods. We stood beneath one of the two Catalpa trees that were planted by Mrs. White back in the early 1900's to mark the entrance to her house. The house had been razed years ago when parkland was being acquired, but the two trees still stood. The catalpa we were under was dead on one side, with one bare, hollow branch that hung out over the road. Suzie sat contentedly while Colonel McLaughlin and I exchanged greetings, and caught up on life since our last encounter.

Smack! With no warning, a large black rat snake landed on the pavement about a foot away from Suzie. Simultaneously, Suzie bleated out a high-pitched yelp and practically jumped up into the tree! Upon returning to Earth, she scampered about wildly, yelping and growling at the snake, that, by this time, was coiled and vibrating its tail. When Colonel McLaughlin pulled Suzie a few feet away, she finally calmed down a bit, but sat whimpering and trembling. Then we assessed the scene to figure out what had happened. Still caught in one of the snake's coils was a small section of bark and, up in the tree branch above us, we spotted a section of loose bark about to drop on our heads. The snake, evidently, had been sunning itself atop the branch when its perch of bark sloughed off and fell to the ground.

As the snake relaxed and unwound, we had a little laugh over what that scene must have looked like from its perspective. Lying there, soaking up the Sun, it had suddenly found itself unceremoniously – and probably somewhat painfully – dumped on the asphalt with a small, enraged creature dancing all around it! Such an unpleasant way to wake from a comfortable nap in the sun!

Black rat snakes are common in Potomac Overlook Regional Park as they are in most places in the mid-Atlantic. They can be quite large – up to 6 feet long or more – but are never a danger to Human Beings unless cornered and threatened. Even then, they can be docile. In addition to the distinctively black adults, we occasionally find eggs or the blotchy gray and black juveniles around compost piles or rotting logs.

I picked up the black snake that had almost fallen on Suzie. Smooth and still cool, it was slow and calm in its movements, despite its recent ordeal. A snake's metabolism is much slower than that of bird, kept in motion by only a small fraction of the Sun's energy required to turn an avian life cycle. Pound for pound, even Human Beings need less energy than birds to fuel our bodies. But we are large and blocky and do not lose our heat well.

Colonel McLaughlin and I said goodbye, returning to our respective lives in which we drove our cars, opened our refrigerators, heated and cooled our houses and carried on other activities characteristic of most other people in this part of the world. To keep the cycles of modern culture turning, we expend huge amounts of energy – far more than any other culture before us, and exponentially more than any other species. Centuries ago, the Sun, our food, fire and falling water were the energy sources that kept culture's wheels turning, but we have since harnessed fossil fuels and, more recently, the energy that holds matter itself together. Viewed from outer space, our planet glows with human-produced light and heat; we have become a planetary force.

Another Surprise

A considerable part of a naturalist's work is conducting educational programs for visiting school groups. This duty has always been a favorite of mine, although I commend classroom teachers who spend entire days, weeks and months with their students – a demanding and stressful job. To arrange field trips to the park, teachers call to reserve a date and time, specify the subject matter they want us to cover, and to discuss other pertinent details. Usually, teachers are easy to communicate with, and only a short conversation is necessary to make a program reservation. There are exceptions, of course.

One afternoon, I received a call from a teacher at a private academy in Loudoun County, 30 miles to our West. The teacher had a British accent and a clipped, insistent manner of speech. He wondered what kinds of programs were available and prompted me to describe them in laborious detail. Finally, after what seemed like an hour of my serving as a programs-and-activities catalog, he narrowed in on a program about birds of prey. He rehashed everything we had already reviewed and insisted on settling every detail of the presentation. "Wow," I thought to myself, "what would it be like to have this bloke as a teacher?!" Then he asked if we had an eagle in captivity.

"No sir," I said, "but we do have a Red-tailed Hawk."

"Ah . . . a Red-tailed Hawk," he echoed, "a magnificent bird. Now . . . I wonder if the number of students we plan to bring presents a problem?"

He seemed hesitant. I asked him how many students he had. "Oh, about 400," he replied.

"Four **hundred**??" I blurted, incredulously. "Sir, we could not handle even half that many . . . we would have to do it in at least 4 or 5 sessions . . . preferably even . . ."

I never finished my sentence for the insistent voice cut in asking "would it be all right if the boys brought their slingshots?"

There was a brief pause and then I sputtered "Excuse me?? Who *is* this?" With that, the laughter on the other end of the line was hearty and loud. I pulled the receiver away from my ear, but knew instantly to whom the chortling belonged. It was Bruce – a good friend, an aficionado of practical jokes and, indeed, a teacher at a local private school. And, quite a good actor!

Bruce is a gifted teacher, researcher and explorer. After teaching in Northern Virginia he went on to another private school in New York, where he started an accredited zoo, built a marsh boardwalk, and rehabilitated an old observatory. He also led expeditions to the Galapagos Islands and other places in South America, and worked in Florida studying forest canopies and as a manager of public lands. We speak only occasionally, but remain good friends, and every so often, he reminds me of the day he had me going.

Among many places Bruce and I used to explore in this area were the rocky shores of the Potomac River just below the park or near the school where he taught. One day, we went in search of a colony of walking ferns – a curious species of fern that spreads by attaching the tips of its leaves to the ground and then growing a new plant at that point. On one of our forays, we had become silent for some time as we skirted the base of a cliff. As I walked, I slid my hand across the cool solidity of the mica schist, and then came to an abrupt stop.

"I like rocks," I uttered.

Bruce turned around, stared at me for a couple seconds, and then burst out laughing. For some reason, my sudden statement of affinity for rocks had struck a deeply humorous chord within him. When his guffaws and chortles finally ended and he ceased shaking and sniffing, he gathered a more dignified bearing. As we continued our walk, a most profound conversation about rocks ensued. We contemplated the idea that "Life is rocks rearranging themselves," our conversation becoming ponderous and philosophical. Several more times that day, however, Bruce lapsed into laughter when recalling my earlier profession of affection for the hard, heavy foundation of our place.

Quarries

To reach the Potomac River from most parts of North Arlington, you must descend from the rolling uplands, at about 250 feet in elevation, down to the tidal waters at about sea level. A series of short streams cut through these cliffs, allowing passage to the river along gentler terrain than by other approaches. Donaldson Run ushers hikers down to the river from Potomac Overlook, while Pimmit Run and Gulf Branch do the same in the mile and a half upstream and Windy Run and Spout Run in the two miles downstream.

In all but Spout Run, the waters of these streams drop precipitously with picturesque waterfalls in their final one hundred yards. Ironically, it is Spout Run that reaches the Potomac in the quietest manner. This stream was so-named because it used to tumble over cliffs and spout out into the river below. Since its naming, the cliffs have been blasted and quarried away, and Spout Run ends its brief downhill sluice with a quiet meander.

During one of my walks down to the river, I accidentally uncovered part of the story of quarries along these Potomac Palisades. As I slid down a muddy slope near the mouth of Donaldson Run, my foot scraped loose a small fragment of ceramic. Upon closer inspection, I found that it was one among many such pieces scattered, along with ancient beer bottles and dozens of oyster shells, just beneath the surface. Although I could not piece the ceramic shards together, the story fell into place when I learned about a small, nearby settlement that no longer exists.

A number of Italian-Americans from New Jersey came to Arlington in the early 1900s to work in the quarries along the Potomac Palisades. They built shacks and a few modest houses on the hillsides of the palisades between Spout Run and Chain Bridge. The settlement was known variously as The Italian Camp, Little Sicily, or Little Italy. According to an old man I met in the Nature Center many years ago, Little Italy had been quite a rough and tumble place. He had been a policeman in Arlington in the 1930s and recalled having to break up several fights in that area. Beer and oyster parties, it seems, had been a regular pastime along the Potomac in those days!

The Italian quarrymen followed in a long tradition of people who made use of the rock of the Potomac Palisades. Native Americans had quarried quartz and steatite (soapstone) from the cliffs for thousands of years for use as projectile points and pots. Quarrying of granite gneiss (locally known as bluestone) began near the mouth of Pimmit Run in the late 1700's. In the 19th century, Gilbert Vanderwerken operated several quarries near what is now the park, followed in turn by the Columbia Sand and Gravel Company and, finally, the Smoot Sand and Gravel Company that operated the quarries until 1938.

Hiking along the shore of the Potomac near the park, one encounters large, rusty boilers that were used to generate steam to drill holes in the rock where dynamite was placed. Near the boilers are the remains of a cement blockhouse that was probably used to store dynamite. One of the local farm girls of the time recalled how the house shook when the men detonated dynamite. She told of tugboats maneuvering barges close to shore so slabs of rock could be loaded in wheelbarrows via a narrow plank. Occasionally, a loaded wheelbarrow and the man pushing it would slip off of the plank and plunge into the river. The building stone was used in many structures in the Washington area, including the Healy Building, just downstream at Georgetown University, and rock rubble was hauled to a stone crusher in Georgetown and used mostly for road-building. .

After the quarries closed in 1938, many of the Italians moved on, but some stayed in the area and Little Italy lingered on for some time. The Conducci Brothers grew flowers and sold them to people in newly created housing developments nearby. In 1957, these aging Italians were uprooted from their homes when the National Park Service built the George Washington Memorial Parkway. A newspaper picture of the day shows the Conducci Brothers and a friend, Philip Natoli, during the eviction. The image of their weather-beaten faces and resigned expressions is etched in my mind, appearing vividly when I contemplate the rock walls and see the overgrown signs of Little Italy.

A Firm Foundation

The rock cliffs of the palisades are of ancient origin dating back to over 500 million years ago (MYA) – about two times older than the earliest dinosaurs. At that time, this area was covered by the ancient

Iapetus Ocean into which sediments from surrounding highlands were deposited. These sediments piled high on top of each other until they were miles deep. Great heat and pressure metamorphosed the bottom layers into rock that was later exposed as the land rose and layers on top were stripped away. The metamorphic rock that now forms the bedrock of Potomac Overlook is mostly mica schist – a sparkly, gray rock that retains the layered look of its marine origins. Other metamorphic rocks with weird and wonderful names such as metagraywacke, gneiss and granite gneiss predominate in other parts of the Potomac Palisades.

Between 450 and 350 MYA, the geologic story of this area began to change quite markedly. Up to this point, it had been one of deposition and metamorphism within a large basin, but the collision of Earth's North American and North African plates now caused the crust to be uplifted, folded, buckled and further metamorphosed. This collision created the Appalachian Mountains, which originally may have been higher than the present-day Rockies.

In Triassic times (about 200 MYA), the continental plates began to pull apart once again. This wrenching of the Earth's crust resulted in enormous splits, or rifts, in the land perpendicular to the direction of separation. Found from North Carolina to New England, these roughly North-South basins filled in with sediments almost as fast as they were formed. The resulting sandstone and shale were red in color due to the oxidation (rusting) of iron. The red sandstone used to build the Smithsonian Castle on the National Mall and many other structures in the Washington, D.C. area came from quarries in the Triassic basin near Seneca, Maryland. With a bit of imagination, one can sense the legacy of an ancient atmosphere from which some of the same oxygen molecules breathed by dinosaurs and strange fishes created these handsome reddish hues. Forces such as those that created Triassic basins also caused faulting and cracking of the metamorphic bedrock in this area. Quartz, which has a relatively low melting point, was injected into these cracks and then cooled to form the white veins found along the Potomac River and in the park.

After the two continents split apart, seas once again inundated this area. About 100 MYA, during Cretaceous times, the lapped against shores as far West as the present site of Washington, D.C. The Atlantic Coastal Plain, a geologic province extending from New York to Georgia, is made up of the loose, unconsolidated sediments that these ancient seas deposited from the Cretaceous period until the present time. The boundary between the Atlantic Coastal Plain and the harder, crystalline rocks of the Piedmont Plateau to the West is called the Fall Line.

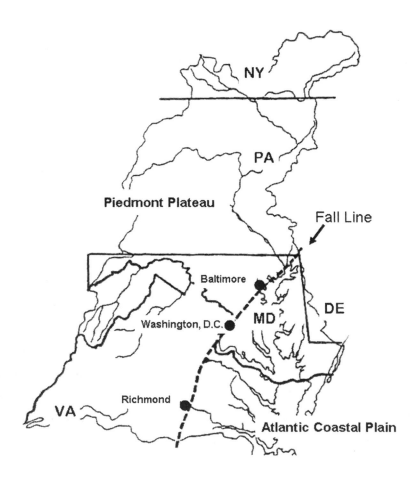

The waterfalls of the Fall Line were created when streams and rivers from the Piedmont stripped away the softer rocks of the coastal plain. Major cities such as Washington, D.C., Baltimore, Maryland and Richmond, Virginia were established along the Fall Line because water-power was available there and because the line represents the highest navigable waters of major rivers. Also, settlements situated at the boundary between two geologic provinces had easy access to the unique resources of both areas (in contrast to settlements well within one or the other province). Potomac Overlook Regional Park is located on the palisades of the tidal Potomac just below the location of the Fall Line. Ancient events of Earth directly affect our Human existence; our story is a long one.

The last one to two million years in the Earth's history (known as the Pleistocene Epoch) were marked by repeated glacial episodes. As the polar ice caps have grown and shrunk, the level of the oceans has alternately fallen and risen by as much as 350 feet. When the last ice age was at its zenith, approximately 20,000 years ago, the Atlantic Ocean was so low that the present-day Chesapeake Bay did not exist. The Potomac River flowed fresh and furious past the area that is now the park, and emptied into the ancient Susquehanna River that flowed where the main stem of the Chesapeake Bay now lies.

As recently as 10,000 years ago, the area that is now Potomac Overlook Regional Park was still under the influence of the ice age and was a mixed evergreen woodland and tundra supporting big game including bison, bear and perhaps mastodon. Various stone projectile points found in the Washington, D.C. area give evidence that Human Beings came here during that time to seek the large animals for their sustenance. As the climate warmed, temperate forests once again blanketed what is now the Eastern United States, polar ice caps melted and sea level rose, forming the modern Chesapeake Bay, including the tidal Potomac.

The Outcrop

At a bend in the trail, near the park's boundary with the Dover Crystal neighborhood, is an anomalous outcropping of large, white quartz boulders. Common as small, loose stones in the park, this mineral – silicon dioxide – rarely shows itself in such impressive form. The outcrop is but a small surface portion of a large dike that formed when molten quartz shot up through a crack in the bedrock. Continental shifts and the buckling of land along fault lines result in such mighty injections. Hiking along the steep palisades of the Potomac, one occasionally encounters a white stripe of quartz extending up the rocky cliffs. The outcrop is the continuation of one of these dikes. Its boulders range from about one to three yards across – massive for quartz – and present themselves like a small stonehenge as if arranged by ancient beings for some ritual or celebration.

One afternoon, while returning from the far end of the park, I came around that bend in the trail and upon four young men in their late teens or early twenties sitting at the quartz henge. They were quiet, almost serene. One fellow greeted me with a simple "hey." Another, absorbed in his cigarette, let out a long, slow exhale, watching the smoke swirl like a ghost above his head.

The scene might not have been as memorable but for the fact that after work, a couple of hours later, I went jogging through the woods and encountered the same young men again. So far as I could tell, they had not shifted an inch from the places I had seen them earlier. They sat placidly and the same fellow who had spoken before offered me another laid-back greeting.

I took notice of the young men, now, wondering about their lingering presence. However, there was nothing suspicious, no attempt to hide anything. The young men's eyes were clear and alert. It seemed that they were simply content to hang out among these rocks and enjoy the beautiful afternoon and evening. This I could understand, for I had done the same on occasion. I like the outcrop's geologic story, the look and feel of the place and the mysterious effect it sometimes has on me. (Recall that I like rocks!) The blocks of quartz exert a curious attraction, compelling me to sit in quiet contemplation. In the few seconds it took me to run past the quartz outcrop, I traded an unspoken appreciation with the four young men and the scene was etched into my mind. The rocks tell stories and sometimes we listen.

Sasha and the Snow Cat

Making snow-sculptures is a Winter pastime that I have enjoyed over the years. Sometimes alone, sometimes with a staff member or friend, I heap up large, compact piles of snow and then use shovels, knives and other tools to carve out animal or Human figures. Over the years, we have created snow squirrels, lions, turtles, a bust of Mozart, and even a figure posing like Rodin's "The Thinker" on a toilet! A passer-by wondered aloud, "what's that? What's that he's sitting on . . . ?" Then laughter. "The stinker!" another person blurted out, "it's the Stinker!"

One morning, while I was upstairs in the Nature Center office, vicious barking and growling suddenly broke the silence. I peered out the window and beheld an amusing scene – a large German shepherd, teeth bared, was straining mightily against its leash, intent on attacking a snow cat that we had built the previous afternoon! The snow cat was about 7 feet long, but very life-like. The dog's owner was holding the dog back with all of his might yelling "No, Sasha! No!" Sasha was bent on sending this huge, obstinate, white cat to its maker, but little did she know that its maker was watching the drama unfold!

The powerful dog steadily dragged his incensed owner toward the colossal cat. Finally, Sasha came close enough to where she could have slapped the poor feline's head off with one swipe of her paw. However, she then suddenly became cautious in her stance and started sniffing at the base of the snow cat. After a few seconds, she evidently concluded that this strange, white cat was perhaps real and of great danger, for she turned tail and started to lurch away from the awful snow beast, yapping and panting!

Sasha's owner had sought to keep her away from the snow sculpture, but now seemed even more miffed that his dog was afraid of the frozen feline. He pulled on the leash, back towards the sculpture, seemingly trying to reason with Sasha that she shouldn't be such a "fraidy cat." At this point, I had to pull my nose off the window and withdraw to the middle of the office lest my laughter be heard below. After having been reprimanded for her aggressiveness, poor Sasha was being branded a coward.

More than just a good chuckle, the memory of Sasha and the snow cat brings to mind to the wonder of awareness – how perceptive all forms of life are of their surroundings. Notwithstanding errors in perception, which we all – like Sasha – occasionally suffer, all beings know their surroundings through myriad senses that keep us from bumping into things, compel us towards food and beauty and keep us alive! For instance, when I walk down my driveway, Mourning Doves perched on the telephone line above me know my actions and even perceive my intentions (rightly or wrongly)! If I look at the birds out of the corner of my eyes, they usually remain perched placidly on the line. But, if I turn and face them directly, they become visibly nervous and often fly away. Insects find their way to food and mates by sight and smell, drawn by color and pheromones. Scientists have even found that trees are aware of their world in a variety of remarkable ways. Not only can they sense light, water and other things they need to grow, they also perceive gravity, chemicals emitted by soil fungi, and even airborne chemicals produced by other trees in response to insect infestation! Living beings can sense danger and safety, polarized light and changes in air pressure, magnetic fields and even time. We are, all of us, linked to the rest of life by a web of connections, visible and invisible; known and unknown; we are *aware*. I am even connected to Sasha and the snow cat by a sense of humor, and that awareness makes me laugh!

Other Residents

As often as possible, I take a walk to start the day, loosen my joints and see what I can see. Whether bundled up and toting a cup of coffee on a cold, Winter day, or dressed only in sandals and shorts in the heat of August, I always head off with a sense of curiosity. My usual route starts down a steep path, about a hundred yards from my house, which descends to Donaldson Run.

Early one morning as I headed down towards the stream I chanced to look up the hillside above the trail when a movement stopped me in my tracks. On a step-like landing below a foot-wide hole in the hill were three foxes – an adult standing behind two young pups. All three stood stiffly, ears up, and stared intently and directly at me. My sudden stop heightened their level of alertness, but they did not budge from their earthen perch.

The foxes and I stared, unblinkingly, at each other for a couple minutes, but then something remarkable occurred. The two kits began to glance away, yawn and even began pawing playfully at each other. At first, they frolicked tentatively, stopping every few seconds to look back my way. As time went on, they seemed quite unconcerned about my presence. They batted at each other, rolled and somersaulted, even growled a bit. The adult fox kept its eyes on me for the duration, but it, too, had relaxed noticeably. Occasionally it nipped or licked its two little ones. Even when I finally turned to continue on my walk, all three paid me only a moment's notice before returning to their play.

The presence of these shy, usually nocturnal, wild canids indicates a fairly intact habitat with sufficient food, water, shelter and space. In some places, it also demonstrates Human *tolerance*, for the red fox can often live in suburban areas so long as it is not trapped or poisoned. Whether in woodlands or suburbs, foxes add a layer to the pyramid of Life's energy. They are omnivores, eating plants and animals in more or less equal proportion – at least in Summer and Fall, when they dine heavily on berries and fruit. Every October, we find large numbers of fox droppings chock-full of persimmon seeds. Foxes also feed on squirrels, mice, chipmunks and other small mammals. I once came upon a fox pouncing and digging frantically until it scurried away at my approach. When I arrived at the place that it had been digging, I saw movement in the loose soil. With a quick scoop of my hand, I sent a mole flying! Ruffled, but not eaten, the silky, paddle-footed insectivore quickly scurried back and dug itself back into its trail.

Foxes add a few strands to the rich tapestry of my own life. Their adaptability instructs me. Their metallic, nocturnal barks thrill and captivate me. When it snows, I look for their distinctive tracks, straight as an arrow with one foot in front of the other. I am amused by the propensity of foxes to gather tennis balls from nearby courts and take them to their dens. One day, a co-worker and I found several such balls just outside a den and a few more that had rolled down the hill into the gully below. These and other stories of my place bring and variety and satisfaction to my life.

The Forest

During the Civil War, a ring of forts was built around Washington when it became evident that the Confederate Army was not going to be defeated as easily as President Lincoln had imagined. Potomac Overlook is situated between two of these: Fort Ethan Allen and Fort C.F. Smith. The story goes that 10,000 Union soldiers cleared the path for the Military Road that connected these and other forts. (The road remains and retains that name to this day). Those soldiers did more than simply clear the road, however.

A U.S. Coast and Geodetic Map of the Washington, D.C. area, dating from shortly after the Civil War, shows that a 2-3 mile-wide swath of trees were cut down between and around the ring of forts. Such clearing was standard practice in order to provide a line of sight of approaching enemy troops. On the map, tree stumps serve as symbols for the devastation. A photograph taken at Fort Smith during the war shows soldiers standing by their cannons with a treeless vista behind them. Deep erosional gullies remain as reminders of a time when, treeless, the land yielded to the rain, losing tons of topsoil to the river and the bay.

As a result of wartime activity and clearing for farms, almost all of the trees of the land that is now Potomac Overlook were cut down. However, in the sense that a rose yearns to flower, this land yearns to tree, and tree it does with red maple, tulip poplar, red oak, white oak, chestnut oak, beech, black locust, black cherry, mockernut hickory, boxelder and a host of others. Like fish swimming in and out of marsh grasses, we live our lives in and among the trees of the forest. Even in more cleared, urban areas, we inhabit a land that would erupt in trees if given a chance.

Of course, people have long cleared parts of the forest for their own dwellings and uses. When Captain John Smith sailed up the Potomac River (or the "Patawomeke" as he called it) in 1608, he described dozens of Indian villages along its shores. The villages were clearings with clusters of timber-framed, mat-covered longhouses. By this time in history, Indians had developed agriculture and many of the villages were surrounded by fields. But the thick cover of trees was never far away. In his "Description of Virginia," Smith describes numerous species including oak, beech, cherries, cedar, ash, and others and wrote that "other plaines there are fewe, but only where the Savages inhabit: but all overgrowne with trees and weedes being a plaine wilderness as God first made it."

One of the trees abundant during Smith's time, and even until the early 1900's, was the American Chestnut. This majestic tree often topped 100 feet and its nuts were a staple food source for Native Americans, colonists, bears and other animals. The nuts are tasty and nutritious. The wood was a major building material for the colonists and farmers; many old cabins were made of chestnut, and a number of beautiful chestnut wood floors still survive in older buildings of this area.

About the year 1900, a fungus was accidentally introduced into New York City on imported Chinese Chestnut trees. Just as smallpox and other diseases from Europe decimated Native American populations centuries earlier, this chestnut blight wiped out American Chestnut trees in the wild within four decades. All that remain are small saplings that sprout from old rootstock, only to succumb to the blight.

I sometimes wonder if the forest "misses" the chestnut trees in some sense. If these trees, like others, emitted chemical signals in response to drought and insect attack, or that attracted other forms of life, does the lack of these signals change things? With the passing of the chestnut, seven species of moths that depended entirely on the tree for food became extinct as well. What other connections might have been broken?

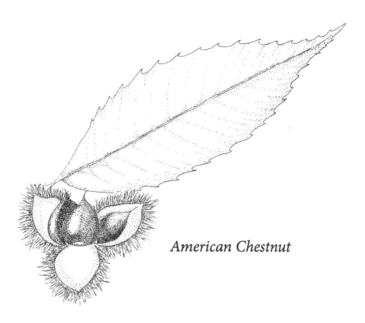

American Chestnut

In the early 1990s we planted five American Chestnut seedlings in the park. All but one was infected with the blight by the end of the decade – their bark blistered with ugly brown welts, and the trees soon died. The resistant tree continued to grow straight and tall with shiny, healthy bark. Perhaps it began to fill the air with pheromones that other trees, insects and the rest of the forest could sense. One night, in a violent windstorm, a large tulip poplar beside the Nature Center tipped over and smashed the chestnut to its stump. A few years later, the chestnut was growing a dozen sprouts from its damaged stump. It, like the land around it, yearns to tree . . . but after a couple years, the sprouts did succumb to the fungus.

A tree that is only present here due to the efforts of Humans is the white pine. Although its usual range is not too far North and West of this area, the white pines in the park were planted by park staff in the early 1970s. The soft, blue-green, flexible needles of the white pine are arranged regularly in bundles of five. (All other pine trees in Northern Virginia, including the Virginia pine, which is found sparingly in the park, have bundles of two and/or three needles.) The needles stay on the twigs for one to two years. White pine seeds are consumed by both birds and mammals, and the needles are occasionally eaten by cottontail rabbit and white-tailed deer. Native Americans ate the inner bark and also used the needles to prepare cough medicine.

The white pine played an important role in our nation's history. Colonists in New England used the large, straight trees for building houses, barns, fences and furniture. The trunks were also prized by the British Navy as ship masts, and competition for the white pine tree was a factor in the Revolutionary War. Staring up the stately trunk of the white pine in front of my house, I wonder why I never learned about this in history class. In high school I did learn that the first Revolutionary War flag displayed a white pine with the subscript "An Appeal To Heaven," but no connection was made to the fact that in the quest to control the riches of the land, we Humans often enter into bitter dispute.

White Pine

The largest and most common tree in the hundred-acre forest is the tulip poplar. Several tulip poplars within the park approach 100 feet or so in height with trunks of about 5 feet in diameter. The awe inspired by staring up the straight, massive trunk of one of these trees is doubled when one considers it tremendous roots, holding tons of wood and leaves steady in the wind. Also known as tulip tree or yellow poplar, the tulip poplar is a fast-growing tree; even though it is termed a hardwood, its wood is actually rather soft. This somewhat limits its commercial use, but it is still an important lumber tree, often used for furniture veneer. We have milled tulip poplars that fall on the park road and turned them into displays in the nature center, furniture and picnic tables.

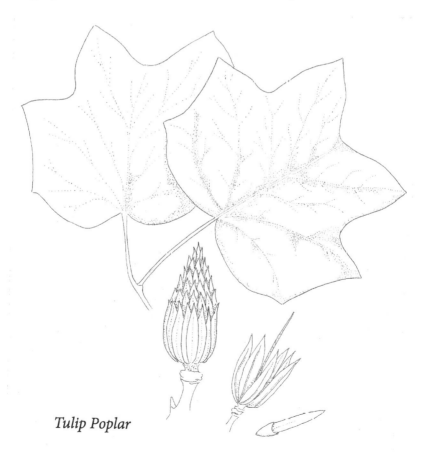

Tulip Poplar

The term "poplar" is a misnomer, for this tree is actually a member of the magnolia family. The greenish-yellow and orange flowers, from which the tulip poplar gets its name, are large and showy and attract swarms of pollinating insects in May, including honeybees from hives behind the Nature Center. Some of the best and greatest quantity of honey is produced during the tulip poplar bloom. Tulip poplar seeds are arranged in cone-shaped clusters about three inches long. Thousands of these seed cones grow on each tree and each cone produces hundred of seeds that provide a Winter food supply for birds and squirrels. Throughout late Fall and Winter, legions of seeds spiral to the ground and can be found practically everywhere in the park between October and May.

With their four pointed lobes, tulip poplar leaves are very distinctive. They can be committed to memory by thinking of their shape as a tulip, a fat, upside-down "T," or the silhouette of a cat's face (the latter, an apt description from a 4th grader visiting with her class several years ago). The leaves have a pleasant, spicy aroma when crushed.

In some parts of the mid-Atlantic, tulip poplars became known as "canoe trees" because Native Americans used their large trunks to fashion dugout canoes. The park staff used a 12-foot section of tulip poplar to demonstrate how dugout canoes were made. We tried, as closely as possible, to duplicate the method of burning and scraping used by the Native Americans. An etching from the late 1500's that depicts two Indians crafting a canoe in this manner shows one of them blowing through a tube (perhaps made of hollow plant stem) to make the fire burn hotter. We found this process to be long and laborious, but were compelled to make creative use of this tulip poplar – the very one that fell close to the Nature Center and smashed our healthy American chestnut!

Homes

For most of my years at the park, I have been fortunate enough to also reside here. My family lives in a red brick ranch house situated at just about the geographic center of the park. It was built by Mr. Dwight Hahn in 1957, about 17 years before the land officially became Potomac Overlook Regional Park. At that time, Mr. Hahn's aunt, Mrs. Fannie White, lived next door in a tiny house located in the midst of what is now the park's landscape garden. Although that house was dismantled when the park was being developed, its sinking foundation is now a neat little nook for a rock garden. Mr. Hahn's house – the one we now live in – is situated on land that was Mrs. White's horse pasture. Across the street, the Deadys lived in the house that was later renovated as the park's Nature Center. Other houses, dating from as early as the 1800's, dotted the land.

Just up the road was a tiny, one-room, one-loft cabin that had been the home of the one of the Marceys (a local farming family) since the 1870's. A cab driver, who had lived in Arlington all of her life, shared with me her recollections of "old Mrs. Marcey" who had lived there. She lamented what a shame it was that the park did not take ownership of the old cabin when it was offered to them. (The cabin was finally purchased by a lawyer in nearby Vienna, Virginia, dismantled piece by piece and reassembled in his back yard!).

Before the farmers, the land had been a backwater wilderness between hubs of activity on the Southwestern shores of the Potomac within what was the diamond-shaped layout of Washington, D.C. Near both Chain Bridge and Aqueduct Bridge (where Key Bridge spans the river now), various mills, cabins, shacks and other structures crowded into the narrow valleys of Pimmit Run and Spout Run. One of the mills near Chain Bridge was reputed to have been used as a storage place for the U.S. Declaration of Independence and the Constitution while the British burned Washington during the War of 1812.

Even earlier, Indians inhabited the land. The Donaldson Site – an archaeological site located within the park – provides evidence that this land was a Spring and Summer settlement for Indians during the period of approximately 500 B.C. to 500 A.D. This was at a time before agriculture, and the Indians lived in small, domed huts covered with bark or animal skins. These wigwams were heated by fire and probably would have been used as shelter only during cold or inclement weather. During the day, people fished, gathered nuts and berries, played games, and made tools and pottery. A fire pit, unearthed during the archaeological dig, was probably used for the ancient ritual of gathering, eating and storytelling. I sometimes try to imagine these people – my neighbors in space but removed by millennia – sitting cross-legged under the stars, staring into the fire.

More than a thousand years later, when Captain John Smith sailed up the Potomac River in 1608, the Indian culture had changed and become more sedentary. Agriculture was, by then, a way of life, at least for the people living in the low-lying tidewater areas of the Potomac and Chesapeake, and houses were larger and sturdier. The longhouses that Smith wrote about, multi-family dwellings that sheltered six to twenty inhabitants, were made with arched saplings spaced along a rectangular floor-plan. A village might hold two to fifty such dwellings, some near each other, some separated by groves of trees. Other written descriptions of Late Woodland villages indicate that large villages had up to 100 houses.

This brief history of Human habitations of this place is the backdrop to the story of the park's only present-day home. My red brick house represents a big departure from all of this land's other Human shelters. It was the first – and is still the only – house that was built to draw almost exclusively upon the outside world in its ability to function as a comfortable dwelling. It was the first house here to be hooked to the utility grid when it was built to supply the energy for heating, hot water and various appliances; all of the previous homes on this land used wood or muscle power for these purposes when they were built. Even those houses that, in later years, used coal were set up to burn wood if necessary.

Copper pipes funneled water into the house and the owners had water for all their needs at the flick of the wrist. Faucets instantly supplanted rain barrels and trips down to the spring. Gravel and asphalt roads soon ensured easy and quick trips to the store. In the mid-1900s, the mule and horse buggies that creaked their way to market with loads of local produce and goods were quickly replaced with trucks and automobiles. These vehicles covered much greater distances in shorter periods of time and carried larger loads of food, fuel and building materials. They also enabled the pursuit of vocations far away from the land on which the house was built.

The only major connection to be preserved between the house and the land was the septic system. Many of the nutrients that flow from the Human activity in the house find their way to the soil, lawn and landscaping out front. But every four or five years, the septic company comes and hauls the sludge away to some unknown repository. I sometimes wonder where parts of my food and parts of *me* have ended up after this purging!

For good and bad, consequential and inconsequential, my house became the first on this land to be, in essence, *removed from* the land. Over the past half century, since the Hahn house was built, Human interactions with the rest of Earth's living system have fundamentally changed. For most people in the United States today, the places we live are not the sources for our food, building materials, or fuel as they once were. Some consider this to be "progress," a step in the right direction. Many probably do not think about it at all.

I moved into the park house with a desire for more direct connections with the land. The garden came first, and a fence was soon added to keep out deer and groundhog. Peas, beans, tomatoes, eggplant, Swiss chard, potatoes and many other vegetables soon grew in the soil just outside my door. I added a rain barrel to provide water for gardening and other uses and to keep torrential runoff during thunderstorms from eroding my back yard.

The simple fact of sunlight shining on my house prompted me to ponder how to make use of the energy of my place. Shades drawn on the East-facing windows kept the Sun out on hot Summer mornings. A solar water heater on the roof transferred the Sun's energy to heat water for washing, bathing and chores. A solar-electric exhaust fan flushes the super-heated air from my attic, reducing Summertime power bills and temperatures in the house.

These relatively small applications of solar energy prompted a larger project for the park's Nature Center. Our staff raised funds to purchase and install a one-kilowatt solar electricity system, which contributes about 15% of our electrical needs. The system is interconnected with the electrical grid, and we continue to count on the local electrical utility for the electricity needs over and above that which is produced by the solar panels. On those rare occasions when the solar panels produce more electricity than we need, we watch the electric meter spin backwards!

When the large fruiting cherry outside the dining room died and started dropping branches on the house, we had it milled into lumber. Some of the furniture in our house was crafted from that beautiful, reddish lumber, and much of the rest of the wood was given or sold to local woodworkers. The large branches from that cherry, or that fall from other trees near the house, are fuel for the wood stove that fits as an insert in the downstairs fireplace. When its cast iron body heats up, the stove radiates tremendous warmth into the house rather than sucking the heat away as a fireplace would. Not only is the warmth provided by the storm-shed branches delightful on a cold Winter night, it is one of the most immediate ways in which I feel directly connected to the land I inhabit. Taking kitchen scraps out to the compost pile also contributes to this sense of belonging. When I work the compost into my garden soil, pea shells become tomatoes, leftover eggplant becomes Swiss chard and they all become me! A home is more than just a shelter, it is a place where we interact profoundly with Life. Properly viewed, it is part of our biology – a living extension of our species.

Even when, as in modern-day homes, we are physically removed from connections with our food, energy, water and other elements of Life, we continue to count on relationships with other people. I relish the company of friends and family, and many wonderful memories are set in my house. It has been a perfect setting for dinners and parties, and rendezvous for walks, hikes and family visits. For many years, two of my out-of-town sisters made a tradition of abandoning their husbands for a week in Spring or Summer to bring their children and spend a week in the wilds of Arlington.

Among my fondest memories are from a Thanksgiving Day long ago. A crowd of friends gathered to help me build a small deck in the backyard and then we cooked and enjoyed a fabulous Thanksgiving dinner. This small version of a barn raising was a blessing that spirals down through the years and connects me ever more intimately with my place. On cool Fall afternoons, the sounds of the saw, hammer on nail and laughter still ring in the air, arriving unbidden along with the faint scent of turkey and dressing.

Music

At another wooden deck, the park's stage, I sat on a chair in the dark and pulled my horn from its case. It was a still night, hushed save for the occasional "beeet" of a nighthawk flying overhead. There was even a break in the jet traffic flying in and out of National Airport. I loosened up the horn's valves a bit and then played a long, trailing note into the night air. The baritone horn's deep, resonant sound filled the grassy amphitheater and disappeared into the woods. I listened to the ensuing silence and then began to play songs that were etched in my mind from decades past and a song I had just played earlier that evening during one of our Summer concerts.

Music has been a big part of the story of this place. Every other Saturday evening during the Summer, the amphitheater comes alive with the sounds of jazz and blues, rock, classical, bluegrass and folk music. The music draws people of all ages. Families and friends lay out picnics on the lawn, older couples set up folding chairs, and children dance and sing to the music or roll down the hill in a nearby play area.

Of course, music does not arise from Human voice and instrument alone. Truly awe-inspiring melodies are performed by the Wood Thrush and the Carolina Wren. Wind in the trees can be hauntingly beautiful as well, a symphony alternating between minor and major keys. In mid-Summer, tremendous choruses of katydids fill the night with their ancient songs. Even the noisy chatter of fighting raccoons and the boom and crash of a falling tree can inspire us in ways similar to musical compositions – they are exuberant emanations of the Life of our place.

Like the Greek muses from which the word derives, music is mystical. Music, brings us together. It can calm and sooth us; inspire and motivate us. These qualities shine through at the park's annual Summer Solstice Percussion Festival, an event that celebrates the longest day of the year and brings a new energy to the park. Although the festival draws young and old, it has conspicuously attracted teenagers who come with their own drums, congas, shakers and rain sticks. Heavy with the beat of these and other percussive instruments, the music seems to conjure up images of the muses, themselves, dancing in the humid air.

The Nature Center

The park's Nature Center is situated roughly at the geographic center of the park, a few hundred feet from the house. It was converted in the early 1970's from a house built in 1912 by George Mitchell who had bought the land from Webster Donaldson. A small auditorium was added for programs and meetings. The Nature Center houses the naturalist staff, holds displays, handouts and other educational materials, and hosts a wide variety of programs, indoor concerts, birthday parties and other events.

One day, a gentleman introducing himself as Mr. Deady came into the Nature Center. He and his family had been the last private owners of the house, just before the property was acquired by the park authority. Mr. Deady gave me a tour of his house, telling me where the living room, kitchen, and bedrooms had been as well as sharing a few stories that occurred in the house. This imparted a very vivid sense of the Nature Center as a human dwelling; every so often, when someone remarks on its homey feel, I relate this bit of its history.

Through the doors of this modest, former home come people of all ages for a varied offering of programs and activities. Four-year-olds, wide eyed and full of wiggles, flock in for the senses program, a chance for them to absorb the world with their eyes, ears, noses, fingers and even their tongues. College groups come to study solar energy. Fourth graders learn about the Fall Line and local geology as required by the state's Standards of Learning. Over the years, hundreds of high school and college interns and volunteers have worked in the park's gardens and trails, prepared handouts and displays, helped with publicity, or simply come to learn about work at a Nature Center. Senior citizens also participate in and sometimes present programs at the center; a traditional Winter Solstice program often features seniors telling their stories about what life was like in earlier days.

The Nature Center is a conduit to the rest of the hundred-acre forest; rare is the occasion when individuals or groups restrict their visit just to the building. Programs sometimes begin indoors with introductory information or activities, but almost always progress to the woods and gardens. Far better to rock-hop over boulders of mica schist than to see, indoors, a detached slab of the oddly named rock. The taste of a freshly picked tomato and the feel of dirt under the fingernails are superior in almost every way to a lesson limited to an indoor discussion of plant micro-nutrients. And watching a fan whir after hooking its wires to a solar electric panel engages the whole mind far better than just an academic discourse about photo-activated silicon wafers.

The Nature Center is also a place for people to understand connections in the world as of which they are a part. The first display in the center highlights the theme: "Everything is Interrelated." At every other display area, whether it be about birds, reptiles or solar energy, people are invited to find connections to other areas of Life. Perhaps one of the most compelling connections to be made is the link between the land and the people who once inhabited it.

The Donaldsons

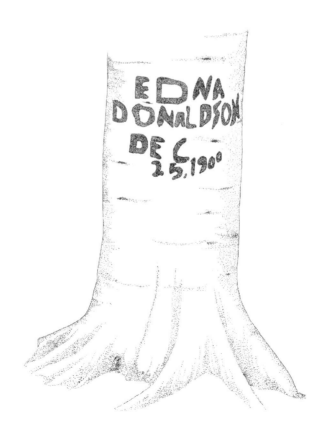

Scrawled in the smooth, gray bark of a beech tree near the edge of the park are the words *"Edna Donaldson, December 25, 1900."* The letters are wide scars stretched by a century of added tree girth. Edna was the daughter of Webster Donaldson, who farmed this land in the early 1900's. I visit this tree every so often and sometimes hear the whispers of people who trod this ground long ago. Almost 100 years to the day after Edna left her mark, I walked down to the tree to commemorate the Donaldson Family's tenure on this land and brought along a copy of our park's field guide to re-read the history chapter at this special place and date. The December day was chilly, and clouds blew along fitfully as if catching on the bare treetops. I sat on a pile of dried leaves beside the tree and began to read. The words conjured up images and memories . . .

On November 2, 1842, Robert Donaldson purchased a 98-acre tract of land formerly belonging to John Mason, Grandson of George Mason who wrote the Virginia Bill of Rights. He and his wife, Ellen Thompson, both grew up on farms in Fairfax County. Their six children, Eliza, Franklin, Ann, George, Hiram, and Webster were all born in Alexandria County [now Arlington].

Robert built a log house and barn on the property. The rock foundation of the barn is still visible. Robert named his farm Fair View. When Donaldson began farming, the trend was toward "market farms." He grew wheat, oats, corn, potatoes, tomatoes, lettuce, onions, strawberries, blackberries, raspberries and rhubarb. Taking the produce to market in Georgetown was a long arduous trip by horse and wagon.2

The family name, Donaldson, is a part of the daily lexicon at Potomac Overlook. "Follow Donaldson Run down to the river," we advise hikers who are looking for directions. The foundations of a few structures in the park still stand as testament to the family. The archaeological site within the park boundaries is called the "Donaldson Site." And now, in the park garden, we still grow some of the crops that these early farmers relied upon. The Donaldsons, who came to this land long ago and who were gone before the land became a park, are still a big part of the story of this land.

After the Civil War, Donaldson filed a claim for damages incurred when Union troops occupied his land at different times during the war. (There were not sufficient quarters to house all of the soldiers. Consequently, soldiers often stayed on nearby farms and some were quite free with the use of their hosts' belongings.) His claim gave a loss of $1,080.00 for cattle and forage. The government paid him $244.20 [About $4,000 in today's dollars]. *Union soldiers left numerous articles behind on the Donaldson farm at the end of the war. Many of these articles were saved and passed down through the Donaldson family.*

Many years ago, a co-worker and I visited relatives of the Donaldson Family who lived about 20 miles away. They had inherited many artifacts that had been collected by the family on their land just after the Civil War and had laid them out on their table for us to see – rifles, swords, belt buckles and all other manner of gear and paraphernalia. Mr. McDonald picked up one of the sabers and unsheathed it, revealing a glistening, sharp edge, untarnished by time. In its polished metal, one could almost see a reflection of the land long ago – stripped of its trees, bristling with military.

Webster was the only son to continue the Donaldson farming enterprise. He grew corn, potatoes, onions, cabbage, tomatoes, berries and dahlias and raised chickens, cows, hogs, geese and horses. Webster and his brother George took the farm produce by rowboat to sell in Georgetown. George was not a farmer. He built houses for about twenty years and did some cabinet making. He also served as Justice of the Peace for Alexandria County.

A family story relates that George liked to fish on the Potomac and often slept between nibbles. On one particular day, when George tied the line to his leg and dozed off, along came a large fish [possibly a sturgeon] that, with a good tug, jerked George into the Potomac. Nearby fishermen came to his rescue. Poor George took so much kidding as a result of this incident that he stopped shopping in Georgetown and instead preferred the long, overland trip to Alexandria.

As I read this story in the field guide, I could not stifle a quiet laugh. I often relay the tale, with the best of humor, during our occasional Heritage Programs at the park. But I sometimes follow it with a fishing story in which *I* was the one left in an awkward position. One morning while a friend and I were fishing at the Potomac, I found a flat boulder beside the water from which to cast. The warm day and lulling sounds of the water filled me with contentment, and I slipped into a trance-like daydream. I was oblivious to everything except the angle and path of my fishing line. Not until my tackle box floated across that line of vision did I suddenly realize I was surrounded by water. The tide had come in with what seemed to be unusual stealth and left me stranded. I had to wade through the water to get back to shore, much to the amusement of my pal.

After Robert Donaldson died in 1887, the Circuit Court of Alexandria County assigned commissioners to partition the land for his surviving children Eliza, George, Franklin and Webster. George Donaldson initially sold a total of 25 acres. He sold a 5-acre lot to George Mitchell in 1907. This sale included water rights to the "Old Indian Spring." Mitchell built a house on this property in 1912, lived in it for some time, and later rented it out. In 1948, he sold the house and property to Emmett Deady.

Mrs. Fannie White of Washington, D.C. purchased 13 acres of George Donaldson's land in 1909. Mrs. White had a very successful apple orchard. At harvest time, she loaded her apples in a wagon and sold them on the streets of Cherrydale.

Mrs. White's orchard can be seen quite clearly in a 1937 aerial photograph on display in the Nature Center. The photo shows the neat rows of trees, a number of homes, and a landscape dotted with farms and scrubby trees. The time lapse of this aerial photograph juxtaposed with others from the 1970s and 1980s brings other history lessons to life. The George Washington Memorial Parkway, built in the late 1950s, is conspicuously absent in the 1937 photo as are the vast majority of houses that now blanket the land just outside the park. The farm plots and shrubby areas that are not built up with houses have now grown back as thick forests.

A close examination of the 1937 aerial photograph reveals another feature long gone. It is a delta of sand formed at the mouth of the stream, now called Donaldson Run, where it flows into the Potomac. The Donaldsons used this as their personal beach, and they called the stream "Swimming Landing Run." The beach may have been deposited by sediments washing down the stream off of the cleared land upstream and/or deposited by a flood on the Potomac. Depending on the season, source and timing of floods on the Potomac, different kinds of sediments are deposited or washed away. After a big flood caused by snowmelt in the Winter of 1996, a small sandy beach reappeared at the mouth of Donaldson Run, but it was quickly washed away by smaller surges of water. I look forward to the day that another flood restores the sandy beach the Donaldsons knew; to setting out a lawn chair and watching the river go by.

In George Donaldson's will of 1919, he bequeathed "two and three quarters of an acre of land together with buildings and improvements to Mrs. White for taking care of me in sickness and paying my doctor bills and funeral expenses and burying me beside my wife in the family burying ground." George died in 1926 at age 90. The Donaldson family cemetery was Northeast of Webster's house on a hillock off Marcey Road. In all, eleven adults and four children were buried in the family cemetery. All remains were moved to Columbia Gardens Cemetery (in Arlington) in 1962.

All that remains of the Donaldson cemetery are a few quartz footstones. A small display plaque at the site features a picture of the burial grounds with a distinctive, four-trunked tulip poplar nearby. This tree still stands as a testimony to the location of the cemetery and is representative of the way in which much of this land's history can be interpreted. An ancient row of locust fence posts still standing in the woods speaks to a time when pigs, goats and horses – not trees – populated the hillsides. Overgrown boxwoods or patches of daffodils mark many of the old home sites. These subtle signs help make the whispers of the land's people loud enough to hear and understand.

South to West

Though engrossed in the re-reading of this history, I was roused by a biting wind and setting Sun. I surveyed Edna Donaldson's 100-year-old writing one last time and then headed back up the hill. Walking briskly back home, I pondered this place . . . .. its land and people, its stories. When I reached my house, I paused and turned back around before opening my front door, shivering with a sense that my place was alive and pulsing with things to say.

The medicine wheel can help us discover this life and pulse of place. At a personal level it tells that each of us is born with strengths and tendencies symbolized by one or two of the four directions. To know ourselves more completely, however, we must travel the Circle of Life and learn and experience the symbolic attributes of the other directions as well. This is a compelling story to me. I think my innate tendencies are towards introspection (the symbolic attribute of the West) coupled with a desire for vision (the attribute of the East). Considering the story of the medicine wheel prods me to pay more attention to developing my strength and endurance, and to become a more nurturing person (the attributes of the North and the South, respectively).

The value of the medicine wheel story (and many similar narratives inherent in circle and four directions motifs, worldwide) extends beyond personal insight and enrichment. The attributes of the four directions are lenses through which we experience the world as well. And, as we continue our exploration of place by turning to the West, we find ways to connect our human consciousness to that of the land..

CHAPTER 2

The West

*Introspection – the land knows
itself through our consciousness.*

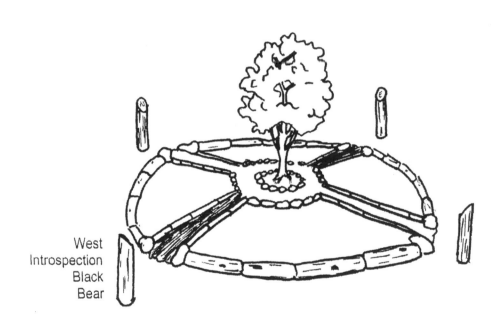

West
Introspection
Black
Bear

West **is the direction of introspection.** Over the years, I
have often visited the Indian Circle Garden in a mood of
reflection, and have seen many others doing the same. A
young woman appeared one day and performed a silent ritual, standing

51

a few minutes at each directional post while looking towards the center of the circle. Various groups have held ceremonies or prayers. People in one such gathering arrived with lawn chairs and sat around the perimeter, saying almost nothing during their stay. A family visited to sprinkle the ashes of a relative over the garden. They, too, said very little, but left with smiles on their faces. One Spring, the circle garden was graced by a youth choir from a church in Fredericksburg, Virginia. Hand in hand around the circle, they raised the hymn, "For the Beauty of the Earth."

When one of the captive birds of prey at the park, "Estelle the Kestrel," died, our staff held our own ritual to bury her in the circle garden. Estelle had broken her wing by flying into a fence at Lorton prison and was found and cared for briefly by an inmate. She was ultimately delivered to us, as a permanently injured bird, by one of the employees at the prison who was related to a former park naturalist. We sometimes called Estelle "jailbird." After almost a decade with us, Estelle died one Fall, and her remains have become part of the Fall quadrant of the Circle Garden. More recently, my wife and I buried each of our three old cats in the circle garden as they, one by one and within a year, passed away. First was Opie, our big, beautiful orange tabby, then L.C. (Little Cat, for short), and finally "Pooh" – the sweetest cat you ever saw. Each of these animals had colored our lives with beauty and radiant intensity, and we wept as we laid their bodies into the Earth.

Stories from *other* places near and far – those of friends, family, park visitors, Estelle, our cats, and even stories from my own life before I lived here – are a part of the character of this place. Before moving to Arlington, I had lived in and experienced many other places. As a child, and to a lesser extent, as a young man, these displacements were not easy, but they enriched my life with perspective and experience.

The stories of my past continue to influence me in the present, especially when I have the time let their goodness and wisdom sift slowly into my consciousness. Since I become more and more a part of my place with the passing years, so too, in a very real sense, do my stories. Through the human mind and heart, the land knows itself.

Stories from Afar

I was born on the other side of the world from where I live now. My parents had gone to South Korea as Methodist missionaries, and my three sisters and I were born in the "Land of Morning Calm." Many memories from that time and place, far away, color my life today and have become part of the story of the land where I live now.

When I close my eyes and recall my earliest years in Korea, I sometimes see children skating on a frozen rice paddy. Their laughter rings as crisp and clear in my mind today as it did in the wintry air so long ago. I see my little friends, their outlines rounded by layers of clothes, making pirouettes around the ice, their breaths clouds of moist steam. I feel my frozen toes. I see a farmer with a string of dead sparrows. Rice stubble catches a skate, making me lurch to catch my balance.

Then, too, I feel my little lungs straining as my sisters, father and I clamber along and over waterfalls of a mountain stream, frozen in space and now in time. My father often took us on hikes into the mountains, and I soaked everything in, not knowing, until years later, how profoundly it would affect me. Even today, I can smell the eggs and meat cooking in a cast iron pan over an open flame next to the frozen white pillows of the icy stream. Later, atop a granite knob on a peak high above the stream, we watched a hawk circling in the mist: a circle of bare rock upon which we stood, orbited by a circle of feathers. This image, more than any other childhood memory of Korea, is ingrained in my memory.

On one occasion, as I watched a hawk circling above my yard in Virginia, a new image suddenly fluttered into my consciousness alongside that of the hawk circling the mountaintop long ago. It was the Korean Flag. Far from being a random or strange juxtaposition, this made immediate sense to me because of the increasing confluence of ideas in my mind. The Korean flag consists of four anagrams, each one consisting of three broken and/or solid lines that symbolize Earth, Water, Fire, and Heaven. The anagrams for the opposite forces of Earth/Heaven and Water/Fire are situated across from each other on the flag with the classic symbol of opposites, the circular Yin-Yang, in the middle.

Although the symbolism of the Korean flag had been impressed upon me at a very early age, its relevance was just now occurring to me. Ancient symbols have enormous bearing on the present and future for they often capture basic truths that transcend time. What the ancients saw in the world – the basic elements, the subtle balances between them – are a large part of what Human life was, is and will ever be about. The modern world brings amazing new insights and changes, but we must not let them obscure or devalue ancient, yet fundamental, wisdom. Heeding my own advice, I pondered the image of the Korean flag in the context of the forest where I now live. How might the symbolism prompt a new awareness of my place? I began with the two pairs of opposites – Fire and Water; Earth and Heaven.

Fire. On average, the Sun shines 56 percent of daylight hours in the Washington, D.C. area. We receive 13.7 mega-Joules of solar radiation annually – which compares to 11.4 in Olympia, Washington and 21.2 in Tucson, Arizona. In plainer terms, this means we have a fair amount of potential for solar energy. One important part of understanding a place is to know its relationship with the Sun. Trees unconsciously *know* their relationship with the Sun, and this is reflected in their ranges, sizes and patterns of growth. We Humans could benefit from the conscious awareness and use of the same information. By studying the inherent energy patterns of the seasons, climate, and other local phenomena, we can better understand and fit into our place. We can construct and situate our buildings to take advantage of the warmth of the Sun for air and water heating (passive solar energy) and use the Sun's rays to produce electricity (active solar energy) to a far greater extent.

Water. As I sat on a bench, the Sun shone down upon me, but clouds and rain were forecast for the next day. Knowing our place also requires us to know its moisture. Our area's seasonal cycles of moisture are reflected in the forms of Life around us. By knowing and planting native plants that are used to this area's 40 inches of annual rainfall, we can minimize the amount of extra water it takes to keep our landscapes healthy and attractive. As with energy, we can fit into our place better and more elegantly if we know its water.

Earth. I rose and took a hike down Donaldson Run, descending steeply from over 200 feet elevation to almost sea level at the tidal Potomac. Potomac Overlook Regional Park is located right at the Fall Line, the imaginary boundary between the higher, harder rock of the Piedmont Plateau to the West and the lower, softer rock of the Atlantic Coastal Plain to the East. The Fall Line influenced the position of many major cities because it is the head of navigation and teems with falling water used for energy in colonial times. Living at the Fall Line afforded easy access to the kinds of resources found in both geologic provinces.

The ranges of many plants and animals coincide with the Fall Line due to differences in soil types, climate and other factors. The land determines much of the story of any place on Earth. How will understanding the geology and lay of our land help us know and fit into our place?

Heaven. This part of the tetrad is not as easily or neatly defined for the word, "Heaven," carries with it spiritual overtones. However, the etymology of a related word – "spirit " – offers some insights. Spirit derives from a Latin word meaning breath and for many ancient people, the sky itself was Heaven. Not knowing how far away the stars were, nor anything about oxygen or other constituents of the atmosphere, they saw the sky as brooding, silent and mysterious, yet also life-giving. Thus, breathing was literally equated to taking in the spirit ("inspiration"), and death came when one gave up the spirit (or "expired").

We may look upon Heaven from the point of view of the ancients or from a modern vantage point, armed with a sophisticated understanding of atmospheric science and astronomy. But either way, we can sense how Life on our planet blossomed forth over tremendous spans of time as a fertile union between the opposites of Earth and Heaven. Take the world of plants, for instance. From photosynthetic algae that lived in the oceans eons ago, plants evolved into myriad species that extended their ranges up onto the land. They, and photosynthetic bacteria, are still our link to the Sun's energy, their greenness a link to the primordial past. They inspire, transpire and store nutrients from Earth and gasses from the heavens. As they grow and change, they reflect the vast number of histories, circumstances and permutations of chance that characterize different places on our planet.

The survey of my place through the symbolism of the Korean flag compelled new research on my part and brought new and old knowledge together in a sensible context. It provoked new questions about energy and new ideas for energy solutions, greater observation of the requirements of plants and animals, and the interplay of various aspects of our lives. And it inspired me to pay even more attention to my past experiences – they were intimately tied to the present in ways I was just starting to appreciate.

A Year of Fishing

Madison, Wisconsin: my 13th year. Treehouses, model rockets, and soccer games were among the diversions that occupied my youthful energy. Mostly, though, it was a year of fishing. Backlit by sunlight dancing on the ripples or glaring off the ice, scenes of countless angling adventures are burned into my memory. Summer evenings at the pier on Lake Mendota; Fall mornings across town on Lake Monona; Winter days spent skating from hole to hole in the ice; Spring leading back into Summer. It was a year of water, scales, worms and monofilament, and its lessons and simple wisdom spiral back through the seasons and years to the present.

Summer

At 8 o'clock in the evening, the swimmers gathered their towels and flip-flops as the Sun started to sink. My pals and I waited, poles in hand, until the last car door slammed and the lifeguard flipped the sign to "Beach Closed - No Swimming." An evening breeze blew away the last whiff of sunblock and barbecued chicken as our footsteps made hollow, resonant sounds on the metal pier. This was our great discovery! After Human bodies vacated these waters of Shorewood Hills swimming area, schools of white bass arrived in vast swarms. Beautiful, silvery fish with black, dashed lines along their flanks. We had tracked down their Summertime haunts, and as we set our tackle on the pier and rigged our lines, we were filled with anticipation. Pinky jigs and Panther Martin spinners were the lures of choice. Their erratic, darting movements seemed to be irresistible to the aggressive fish, and a hit would practically jerk the poles out of our hands. Once the hook was set, the line became a connection not only to the fish, but to all the mysteries in the depths below.

One night, we had come ill-equipped, and the few lures we had were claimed by the lake after only one fish was caught. We talked of leaving, but, after putting our heads together, arrived at a solution. We cleaned and cut the lone fish into strips and used them as bait. "I heard it works," said my buddy, Todd. And work it did; the ravenous white bass were simply unable to resist the shiny, flashing strips of meat of their own kind! This prompted a litany of dark stories about headhunters and other cannibals, and the little fact of Life was stored away in our minds for future reference. As the setting Sun turned the ripples to gold, then silver, and finally inky black, we pulled up our stringers and walked the mile home in the dark, fish flopping at our sides. Our voices and laughter rang out in the night. Upon our return home, we set up shop in the basement, and began the less pleasant part of the night – that of cleaning the fish. However, as the Summer progressed, so did our ability to clean, store and cook the fish we caught, and these activities became almost as satisfying as the fishing itself.

Those Summer nights brought chills, thrills, laughter, and lessons of all sorts. Once, my pal Mike inadvertently stepped off the pier while casting his line. He emerged from the water gasping and sputtering, but still holding his pole. On another occasion, a huge August thunderstorm sent us scurrying off the metal pier and diving for cover. And, of course, there was the worm business.

The worm business kept me supplied not only with bait, but also cash for all my fishing supplies as well. In just one week, I could make almost $5 – an unqualified success! There appeared to be no end to the demand for the big, healthy night crawlers that I harvested from my own backyard, sometimes with the help of my sisters. I stored the worms in the milk-delivery box. Mom didn't seem to mind, and she even saved coffee grounds that I mixed in with the worm's soil to keep them well nourished. I sold them for practically nothing - 25 cents a dozen - and had the laws of supply and demand been swimming around in my head, the price might have soared to twice that. (And my sisters remind me that I might have also paid my employees more!)

The Summer came and went. Fishing, which had begun as a mere hobby, was also informing my young mind in everything from natural history to Human relations to economics. (But I surely didn't know it at the time.)

Fall

With the crisp air of Fall, the swimmers and the white bass left their shallow bay and we young fishermen struck out for other waters. One such spot was the power plant's warm water outlet on Lake Monona. Because it was down by the railroad tracks on the South side of town, our dads had to drive us, so we didn't get there very often. Yet what they lacked in frequency, these trips made up for in colorful experiences.

White bass, and also crappie, perch, and catfish, were attracted to the warm water, and fishermen of all sorts attracted to the fish. The power company built a concrete deck and metal railing around the outlet, and it was crowded elbow to elbow on some days. Old men chewing on cigars traded fish stories with college students and with us kids. One story everyone seemed to have in common was "the big one that got away."

On one particularly crowded morning, my buddies, Todd and Mohammed, and I felt the yearning for more solitude and an itch for exploration. Conveniently located near the water outlet was a quiet little marina with its boats covered and hoisted from the water in preparation for Winter. Peering through the chain link and wood slat fence, we surveyed the situation and discovered that the marina and adjacent property belonged to the Elks Club. After some discussion on the ethics of entering that area, we took a quick, informal vote. Then with our best cooperative effort, the three of us scaled the fence and plopped down into an uninhabited fisherman's paradise! What apprehension we had about being uninvited guests was eased by silly jokes about Elks and Moose and other such hoofed Humans. We made our way down to the boat slips and cast our gaze into the water.

What we saw caused a temporary lapse of both speech and breathing, and turned our eyes into saucers. There, among the water-weeds, lounged the biggest, fattest panfish we had ever encountered. Bluegills. Known as panfish because of their shape, and these fish were the *size* of pans as well! We broke our silence, chattering excitedly like squirrels in a bucket of acorns, and set about our task with practiced skill. In no time at all, we had 3 or 4 of the monster bluegill on our stringers. True to their kind, they each put up a darting, jumping, belly-flopping fight that made our hearts pound. (I have often wondered why it is, exactly, that a fish on the line can prompt such rapt attention and such an intensely gratifying feeling. It seems to me that an affinity for the hunt is hardwired into my brain, for I surely wasn't taught it.)

A chance look toward the Elks Club alerted us to the presence of another Human Being in our private fishing grounds. We, the exalted hunters of monster bluegills had become the hunted, and we had visions of our heads mounted up on wall plaques in the Elks Club. We had our lines and fish out of the water faster than you can say "night crawler" and were on our way! The man did not seem to have spotted us, but if he ever did, he would only have seen our backsides flying over the fence. Safely on the other side, we gathered our belongings and our wits about us and returned to the warm water outlet to show off our catch.

Winter

Ice. The ice was almost two feet thick that Winter and it expanded up onto the shores and against itself at the center of the lake. The screech of ice on ice was, at times, ear piercing. But this vast white wasteland was just another setting for our never ending quest for fish and for satisfying a blossoming curiosity about the world. We knew that our quarry, the northern pike, lurked in the silent world beneath the ice, and we were determined to catch the sleek, big-toothed wolf of the water. This handsome, predatory fish held a mystique for us young fishermen, and we sometimes referred to it reverently by its Latin name, *Esox lucius*, which we bandied about impressively like little professors.

Getting through the ice was a problem. Being poor little kids, we had no fancy ice-augers that the grown-ups used to bore through the formidable frozen barrier. (The worm business was on seasonal hiatus and would not have funded such heavy equipment anyway.) To fish, therefore, we had to become "hole scavengers," chipping away with hammers and screwdrivers through partially refrozen holes left behind by those with augers.

Smaller fish were the food and bait that attracted Esox. A minnow was dangled a few feet down on a wire leader that could withstand the terrible teeth of the pike. The line was attached to a delicate trip-wire that sprang a red flag, alerting us that the minnow had been captured below. We would usually rig about four or five of these lines and flags and keep an eye on all of them. Depending on our success as hole scavengers, this sometimes meant that we had to skate over what seemed to be acres to attend to our lines, but this had the advantage of preventing us from freezing to death!

On one particularly cold day, when it seemed so far below zero that even hole scavenging might fail, we set a couple rigs in a narrow cove that seemed to be less-than-prime pike habitat. Old holes in other places were completely refrozen. With fingers and toes similarly frostbitten, we started skating furiously to counter the numbing cold. After just one loop we were greeted with the welcome sight of a red flag still quivering from having been sprung. I set the hook, felt a tug, and in a few minutes pulled a pike, about two feet long, through the hole. As Mohammed and I congratulated each other, an adult who had set his lines a couple hundred yards away came shuffling over to see our fish and to bemoan his bad luck. Four hours he had spent in this cold without even a bite, he lamented. It didn't seem right to him that a couple of little whippersnappers should come waltzing out and land such a fine fish in no time at all.

The man was unaware that his fortune was about to change, but Mohammed noticed a red flag waving in the wind off in the distance. When this was brought to the man's attention, he uttered a flurry of unintelligible words as he slipped and slid off to the flag with a whole new outlook on fishing. Although we would have preferred tending to our own sets, our curiosity was piqued when the man appeared to be straining and unduly occupied at the hole. So, off we skated to discover just what it was that had attached itself to the other end of his line.

It was quickly apparent that the man had hooked either a very large fish or the lake bottom for whatever it was did not yield to his tug. When instead he yielded to *its* tug, we concluded that it was the former. A strange sight it must have been – two little boys and a middle-aged man scurrying around on the wind-swept ice doing whatever it took to prevent the "big one that got away." I began to hold and gather loose line so that it didn't slip back out through the man's thick, fumbling gloves. At the man's directive, Mohammed rummaged through a box until he found a gaff. All the while, the man continued to snort unintelligible words that steamed out into the frigid air like smoke from a stack.

When sufficient line was gathered and the huge beast neared the hole, all three of us were nearly overcome with excitement. But the man, now silent, wrapped the line around one hand and held the gaff in the other, and at just the right moment snagged the fish by the gills with surprising accuracy. It was a huge pike! We later learned that it was four feet long and nearly twenty pounds – a record for Lake Mendota that year. The prodigious pike, its tremendous toothed mouth and long, blackish green body, hung over a sled on the ice. I recall the scene with a certain sadness, yet it is part of a happy and even beautiful time of my young life. The melancholy of that quiet moment as we stared reverently at the great, dead fish brought balance and depth to a year in which we kids discovered and became a part of the waters and lands of our home. We ate what we caught, learned an ethic of waste not, want not, and followed our young hearts without undue influence from the outside world there on the ice of Lake Mendota.

Spring

With the long Wisconsin Winter begrudgingly giving way to Spring, we boys yearned to get out on the water again. Because the white bass had not yet returned to their Summer haunts, we made use of a neighbor's boat to fish for perch near picnic point. Perch are clever and crafty fish whose jovial yellow and green striped bodies seem to reflect their clownish antics. Quick to the bite, they will make a fishing bobber plunge, only to withdraw with equal speed. If clear water affords a view of the action, you can see the sleek fish attack the bait with the agility and temperament of a flyweight boxer. Most often, it escapes with most or all of the worm, shakes its head like an enraged bulldog, and then swallows the worm with an eye-bulging gulp. On more than a few occasions, perch depleted my night crawler supply and then peered up through the water, wearing what appeared to be a self-satisfied grin.

If perch fishing developed one's sense of humor, it also developed one's patience. In fact, fishing in any season is a study in patience. Patience was born out of mindless immersion in the activity at hand, as when we concentrated with keen intensity on the bobber and readied ourselves for yanking the line at precisely the right time. Patience was nurtured by the mindless enjoyment of good company as we joshed and joked, and shared boyhood thoughts as the reels went clickety-click. And patience was exercised and kept strong by long stretches of heat, bitter cold, or fish not biting to be endured – preferably mindlessly.

As a new Summer approached, we were mind*ful* of the end of school and impatient for it to arrive. But although we were eager to return to Shorewood Hills swimming area, we bided our time. Each season held its fullness and opportunities for fishing and we followed that rhythm. A year in the lives of three young fishermen was circling into another, its experiences blending imperceptibly with the years that followed.

* * * * * *

I do not go fishing as often as I did in my youth, but the skills and movements instantly return to me when I get the chance to cast a line. Similarly, other experiences and wisdom from those years of fishing color and inform my life here and now in the woodlands of Northern Virginia. I reel in lessons on Human nature, relations and economics as well as insights into the living system of which we are a part. And occasionally, when I do land a bass, perch or catfish from the Potomac, memories of well-spent childhood days dance before me on the water. How important it is for children to be able to explore and absorb the power of the places they live in and grow up! Our pasts become our present, and our lives become part of the land.

Stone Mountain

Stone Mountain, Georgia, was a central part of my life during the several years my family lived in Decatur, near Atlanta. A more striking and monolithic center there could hardly be, for Stone Mountain is the largest exposed chunk of granite in the world, rising 825 feet above its surroundings, about 2 miles long and ½ mile wide. Most of the rock's surface is unvegetated – sheer cliffs or lightning-pocked fields of granite. Where the slope is not too great and not too exposed to the elements, however, colonies of grasses, herbs and trees cling.

The mountain lent itself – inherently, and almost eerily – to my unfolding idea that a sense of place could be enhanced through the circle and four directions motif. I was coming to realize that this motif had been a recurring theme in my life even before I was aware of it. My memories from Stone Mountain, like those from Korea, Wisconsin and other places, have intertwined with my life here at the Fall Line on the Potomac River in some very surprising ways!

Stone Mountain is surrounded by a circular road that links the huge rock's four very distinct sides. The South side has the park's largest expanse of forest, and its secluded lakes, hold even more of my childhood memories of fishing. On the West side is a historical museum and access to the only walking route up Stone Mountain. I have made the 1.3-mile walk up the mountain with family and friends on many occasions through the years, and it was an occasional training run for my high school basketball team. The North side is replete with sporting, eating and other tourist destinations. This includes the huge carving for which the mountain is famous. Three giants of the Confederacy during the Civil War are set in the stone of this North face: Jefferson Davis, Robert E. Lee and Stonewall Jackson, each on horseback. (This grand work was begun in the early 1920's by Gutzon Borglum, who later became famous for carving Mount Rushmore.) Stone Mountain's East Side was its quiet side but, interestingly, the direction to which thousands of those who reach the top from the West would gaze for inspiration. On a couple of occasions, I was part of the throng that climbed the mountain for Easter Sunrise service and looked symbolically to the East for new beginnings.

A little-known story about the top of Stone Mountain offers another link between this great rock and my understanding of place. Although based in fact, it is shrouded by time and garbled by misinterpretation and its resolution was literally blasted apart and carted away! I became aware of this story many years after leaving Georgia, and, despite its fable-like quality, have been fascinated by its links to my life in Virginia.

An early account of the mystery at the top of Stone Mountain comes from a remarkably literate twelve-year-old boy named Francis Goulding.

He visited the mountain with his father and an Indian guide in 1822 and wrote an account that included the following:

> *Encircling the summit, at a distance of nearly a quarter of a mile from its center, was a remarkable wall, about breast high, built of loose, fragmentary stone. . . . the only place of entrance was by a natural doorway under a large rock, so narrow and so low that only one man could enter at a time, by crawling on his hands and knees.*

Goulding, who later became a preacher, novelist and inventor, explained the wall as a military fortification, but this explanation has been questioned and mostly discounted. The wall was not very high, was easily dismantled, and did not enclose a habitation or stronghold. Willard Neal, who wrote a visitor's guide to Stone Mountain, envisioned a religious or ceremonial significance to the stone circle.

> *Consider, too, the old medicine men's penchant for human sacrifice. At dawn the frenzied crowd probably hurled some luckless victim over the rim, while the women and children, who had waited below all night to see the poor devil fall, screamed and cheered, feeling sure that the gods would be so happy about the whole thing that they would assure bountiful crops and good hunting.[3]*

(Neal's style might be dismissed as "antiquated," but it is in keeping with an unfortunate tendency to neutralize the wisdom of entire societies with a blather of words. Rather than discounting our ancestors from many lands as "savage," we might find amazing insight if we took a closer and less prejudiced look.)

Neal then describes the Devil's Cross Roads, a feature at the top of Stone Mountain that he calls "surely as impressive as the great wall."

Devil's Cross Roads was a huge, flat boulder, some 200 feet in diameter and five to ten feet thick that was perched approximately in the middle of the mountain top. The gigantic boulder was split into four equal quadrants by breaks that ran at right angles to the center. One ran "directly north and south, the other east and west." The breaks were small near the periphery of the great boulder and widened to about four feet wide and five feet deep near the center. The mystery of the mountain deepens.

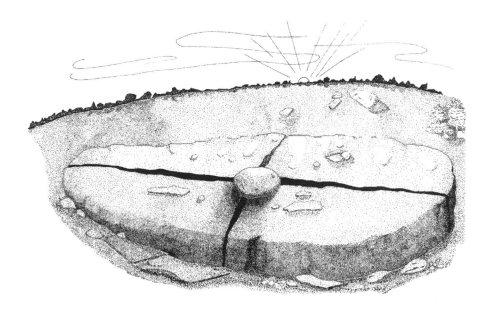

Perched atop this giant slab of rock, right at the center, right over the intersection of the two breaks, was another flat rock. This rock was about twenty feet in diameter. According to Neal,

> "the Cross Roads became a favorite spot to have breakfast for parties who climbed the mountain to watch the sunrise. It was said that everyone wondered that Nature could make a compass as accurate and a great deal more spectacular than the ancient Egyptians could do. The entire formation disappeared in

1896 when quarrymen found that it was composed of superior building stone and broke it up and let it down the mountain by winches."

The owner of Stone Mountain at the time, the Southern Granite Company, shipped the rock to places far and wide, including to Washington D.C. Sometimes when I walk up granite stairs or consider the granite walls of various buildings in Washington, D.C., I wonder if they might have come from the mysterious, circular slab of rock atop Stone Mountain. The story of the circle and four directions has seldom been so literally blasted away. In our modern rush for *progress* and *efficiency*, we have often done an even more effective job in erasing such stories from our day-to-day life.

Four Corners

College years took me first to Emory University in Atlanta, then to Colorado State University, where I received a B.S. in Wildlife Biology, and finally to Virginia Tech to earn a M.S. in Wildlife Science. My time out West began to instill in me a sense that there was much more to our planet than I had been taught in school. What my direct experiences were teaching me about Earth seemed to coincide more with my instincts than with my education. Ironically, this new sense of Earth arose, in large part, as I discovered some of the *ancient* stories of the circle and four directions. During a trip to the Four Corners area (where Colorado, New Mexico, Utah and Arizona meet), I started to grasp the similarity among circle symbols world-wide. How fitting it is, that my first in-depth introduction to the circle and four directions motif should have come from the Four Corners region.

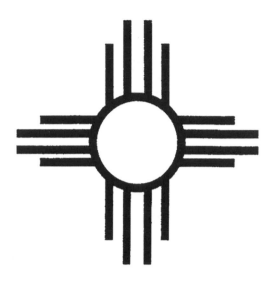

Have you ever noticed the emblem on a New Mexico license plate and state flag? It is the Sun symbol of the Zia Indians of New Mexico. It reflects the ancient tribal philosophy of these Native Americans – the basic harmony of all things in the Universe. The number four is sacred to the Zia Indians because most things they receive from what they call the "Giver of All Good Things" come in fours.

Accordingly, the Sun Symbol has four sets of four spokes radiating from a circle. The sets of spokes represent the four seasons of the year, the four periods of the day (sunrise, noon, evening and night), the four directions of the Earth and the four stages of Human life (childhood, youth, adulthood and old age). Everything is connected by the Circle of Life and Love that has no end and no beginning.

One can sense the timelessness of the Zia Sun Symbol in the land of New Mexico. Numerous Indian pueblos, although affected by modern society, stand as testimony to an ancient perspective on Life. Zia Pueblo has been inhabited since about 1250 A.D. Another pueblo, Acoma, has been continuously inhabited since at least 1200 A.D. – longer than any other settlement in North America. Perched on a sandstone mesa 400 feet above the surrounding flatlands, Acoma affords an inspiring view of other mesas, hills and of 11,700 foot-tall Mount Taylor to the North. The landscape speaks of millions of years of change but also of incredible underlying stability. As I feasted my eyes upon the mesas and mountains and breathed in the crisp, desert air, it felt right that from this place had sprung a symbol and story both unique and universal.

* * * * * *

After finishing my undergraduate degree out West and graduate school in the East, I worked for five months on a Bald Eagle research project on the Chesapeake Bay in Maryland. By this time, the idea that individual places hold powerful lessons for the Humans that inhabit them was starting to take hold in my mind. I also came to realize how the stories and experiences of my past profoundly affected my present *and became part of whatever place I lived.* This realization grew stronger one day on the Chesapeake.

The Shear Pin

Pastel pinks and oranges gently brush the river as the Sun, still unseen, promises to rise on the Eastern Shore. The tranquil scene is punctuated only by a fish breaking the surface or the cries of a gull flying through the mist. A gentle wind, strengthening with the coming day, drives small waves whose sound upon the shore can be heard even out here on the open water. Far away, the wheezy engine of a tugboat beats out a pulse felt in the heart more than heard, and the barge it pushes moves like a ghost up the bay.

But tension accompanies the calm. Everywhere there is tension, because that is how Nature works. Tranquility is the mirror-image of tension, and one does not make sense without the other. Life is characterized by a never-ending cycle of stress and release. Without the stress, nothing would happen; without the release, Life would break down. Hunger, indecision, Summer heat, and shifting plates of the Earth release themselves by eating, laughing, thunderstorms, and Earthquakes. Then satiation, comfort, cool evenings and stillness return . . . . only to give way once again to new stresses.

My mind was absorbing the sensations of morning as I guided the small motorboat through the pilings of the railroad bridge and out into the open waters of the Bush River. Hollow, watery echoes under the bridge gave way to the wild, soulful sounds – and silences – of the river, and I zipped my jacket up an extra inch to keep out the damp chill. The 5:30 Amtrak had passed over a few minutes earlier on its way to New York and other such complicated places. The clatter on the tracks was overwhelming, but it left like a heavy sigh, opening the senses to the underlying rhythms of the tides. A leaf spiraled out of the sky as if dropped from heaven.

My job was to catch an eagle, and I was running late. Always a tricky business, eagle-trapping was best done early in the morning, and, if the traps were set before the Sun came up, all the better. That way, the big birds would not be out of their roosts yet to catch a glimpse of your puttering around on the sand spit. If you didn't beat the Sun, you would often feel the looming presence of an eagle as it soared over and landed in a tree not far away. When this happened, the birds would usually stare down suspiciously at you, and the bait-fish on the sand would sit untouched. Their bird brains served them well. The way things were going, I wasn't going to have the last trap set before the first rays of light brightened the tree-tops. This was not a good thing. The Virginia Tech eagle research team had had poor luck in the last couple of weeks catching our subjects of study, and, as a result, we had a dearth of data. I felt a sense of duty, even a little guilt, and was determined to make the best of the late start. Leaving the trestles behind, I gunned the motor and raced to my destination.

A shear-pin is a small, metal dowel an inch or so long and about 1/8th of an inch thick. It fits neatly into a groove where a motorboat propeller attaches to the driveshaft (or in any number of other types of machinery where it is needed). The shear-pin's purpose is the release of tension. A furiously spinning propeller will be destroyed if it hits a large, immovable object, and with rocks, logs, and other such things lurking in the shallow waters of the river and bay, your motorboat prop will likely be mangled. If it weren't for the shear-pin, that is. If the prop *does* hit something hard and immovable, the shear-pin breaks first and the prop, and perhaps the driveshaft too, is saved. I have had shear pins break on me before. When it happens, I just raise the motor, remove a cotter pin, pull the propeller off, replace the shear pin, re-attach the propeller, and things are back in running order. The whole operation takes about a minute; very simple.

The boat sped on. I had it all planned out. I would only put out one set of traps that morning. Four fish waited in a bag at the top of the cooler – just enough for that set. I would pull the boat in on the deep side and wade ashore in order to make a fast get-away, and I'd work quickly. The boat was flying across the water now, slicing through the waves like a knife. The fiberglass hull hummed with the speed, and water droplets quivered as they slid down the dash onto my knees. My hair was blown back and my jaw was set with the beginnings of a grin. I'd beat those eagles out of the roost yet!

Wham! There was a loud, dull thud and the boat lurched, hurling me forward. My chest hit the wheel, and coolers and tackle boxes tipped, slid, and scattered all over the boat. There were a few moments of mayhem, and then . . . and then there was nothing but the gentle rocking of the boat on the waves. The high whine of the engine was replaced by the plunk of a tern hitting the water and the heart sounds of the far-off tugboat. From my mouth, expletives flowed freely, as I reacted to my sore ribs and to the realization of what had happened. I pounded the dash, causing the water-droplets to jump and dance. "Damn shear-pin!" I yelled out loud. The boat continued to rock gently. I jumped up from the seat and sidled back towards the engine, looking at it with a scowl. "Why did this have to happen *now*?" I thought, "Every minute counts, and those eagles are probably starting to stir right this minute!" I imagined the spreading of magnificent wings and the ruffling of feathers. The engine sat there, impassively, mocking my frustration. A tern hit the water again, this time rising with a fish in its bill. The Earth continued to spin and the Sun continued to rise.

There was only one thing to do. I raised the motor and removed the propeller. Sure enough, it had a jagged nick in it and the shear-pin was broken. "Not a problem," I thought as I reached for the tackle box and opened it to get an extra shear-pin. "I'm getting pretty good at this. It'll only take a few seconds."

The shear-pins were not in their proper compartment. "Must have been knocked out when the box fell." I pulled some plastic bags out of the lower tray. "What the . . . ?" No shear-pins in the lower tray. No shear-pins in the bottom of the box. In fact, there were no shear-pins in any of the tackle boxes. I threw the last box down in disgust. This was not my morning! First the late start, then the damaged prop, and now this! "What am I going to do now? It'll probably take me an hour or two to drift ashore. Even when I *do* hit land, it'll take me another hour to get back to the marina and get help."

My mind raced with all the possibilities as I scanned the river for a fishing boat and tried to judge the direction and speed of the wind.

"There goes catching anything today. In fact, there goes half the day," I lamented to myself. "Damn!" My frustration was complete and I hit the dash again with my fist. As if responding, the engine dropped from its lifted position with a startling thump. The surprise sent me reeling and I almost fell out of the boat. Recovering, I sat down buried my face in my hands, and shook my head. A wind gust gave me a shiver. A shear pin's purpose is the release of tension, and yet, at this moment, it was the *cause*.

I looked up and re-assessed the situation. There was no danger. It was a nice day, if a little breezy and chilly. I had no paddle or oar, but the boat was drifting toward the Southwestern shores of Aberdeen at a fairly good clip. What could I do? Not much. So I sat back in the chair and waited. A gull laughed at me. Feelings of duty, responsibility, and plain old boredom crept in, but my brain fought back with reason: nothing much could be done, and that's all there was to it. I relaxed just a little. The dark form of an eagle graced the horizon.

The to-and-fro of a boat on the waves and the feeling of wind on the face have the ability to speak if one listens. The slow, constant arc of the Sun and the unpredictable billowing of clouds are part of this language. The cries of birds and popping sounds of fish at the surface, and the deep, underlying silence . . . The language speaks in terms of everything and in terms of nothing. It demands to be heard by all of Life, and yet it *is* all of Life, and has not a care. It is an unplanned symphony. The pastel pinks and oranges, ghost-like forms far off in the mist, tension and release – they all have the ability to speak if one listens. But rarely do we listen. Rarely do we afford ourselves the opportunity to listen. We are in a hurry, caught up in a wave of time.

The wind gusts came and went, producing a rhythm of waves lapping against the hull of the boat. Faster, then slower, faster, then slower. My breathing followed suit and a little later, my mind sensed a connection. The Chesapeake was breathing! Its breath flowed in and out of the river, capturing and controlling my breath, until I thought about it. The treetops, ablaze with sunlight, distracted me, and my breathing returned to the rhythm of the wind. My mind recalled bright, fiery scenes of a mountain forest ablaze with fire, not sunlight. Water lapping against the boat doused the memory. Faster, then slower, faster, then slower, the Chesapeake was breathing! It was alive! Subconsciously, I rejoiced and reveled in the possibility. Time disappeared.

The language of the Earth is like fresh water to a person lost on the salty sea. A long draw on the canteen is a pleasurable release from the powerful thirst that beckons. But, in time, the water, laden with other elements of our bodies, flows back out and is used by the rest of Life. Likewise the fast-flowing rivers meet the tide and circulate, eventually becoming one with the ocean. Does the Bay experience pleasure? Does it have a thirst? Earth speaks with timelessness; there is movement and there is change, but in ever-recurring moments. Rivers flow and the clouds form in a never-ending cycle of ever-recurring moments. The self-awareness that produces knowledge of time is a tangent to the circular language of the Earth. Timelessness creates an unplanned symphony; self-awareness *writes* one for orchestra and soloist.

Time had disappeared as had my self-awareness. My body was adrift on a river of water and my mind on a river of unconsciousness flowing directly from the Earth itself. It was like being in a dream where you realize the dream, but haven't identified yourself as the dreamer. I enjoyed Life as I unconsciously joined with it. The sunshine came and went, highlighting the waves, the veins on my hands, and the texture of the floor of the boat. And then from the floor of the boat came a tiny, shiny reflection that burned itself into my mind, and everything changed.

I looked away, not wanting to break the spell. "It couldn't be the shear-pin," I thought. But the thought itself broke the spell, and my gaze returned to the floor of the boat. It was, in fact, a shear-pin shimmering there in the sunlight. Just as it would allow the propeller to spin once more when placed in its groove, the pin entered my consciousness and set my thoughts spinning. The peace that I had settled into while adrift on the river was shattered by a simple awareness. I was now aware that there was a shear-pin in the boat and I could not wish it away. I could not just jump back into the river of timelessness and feel at my core the Life of the world around me. At least not at that moment. I considered tossing the pin into the murky Bush River, but knew that that would accomplish nothing. The awareness of that act itself would prevent my being able to re-enter the spell.

Tension and release. For the Human Being, this law of Nature includes time and timelessness, and the drifting in and out of self-awareness. Our minds spin furiously to do good, to accomplish, to reach a destination. Overwhelmed by the ticking of the clock, we race off on a tangent, away from the Circle of Life. And just when we reach our greatest speed, we will encounter the large immovable objects, the limits, of our existence. Will we crash and break up, or instead take our pause and rejoin the circle? Do we have a shear-pin to release the tension, to tell us what is enough and when to stop and return? Pastel pinks and oranges gently brush the river as the Sun, still unseen, promises to rise once again.

* * * * * *

Stories and lessons from our past are part of our character and being and they become part of places we live. My fishing expeditions on Wisconsin lakes, hikes in Korea, reflections on the Chesapeake and every other part of my past have become part of the land I now inhabit. Like the Wood Thrush that migrates from South America and brings its flutelike song to these woods, I alit on this land and shared my life with it. I am a reflection of this place and it of me.

Silence

Perhaps the biggest annoyance about living and working at Potomac Overlook is the jet noise. We are situated roughly under the flight path to National Airport, about 6 miles away, and the jets sometimes roar overhead. (The volume used to be almost mind-numbing at times; even now, the much quieter jets still can drown out a conversation for a few seconds.) On these occasions, it is hard to be introspective. The world of speed and whining engines forces itself upon you and diverts attention.

Then one day, in 1996, it snowed. And snowed and snowed. Sixteen inches of beautiful, wind-driven powder. A high of 15 degrees. And total silence save for the wind in the trees! For the first time in many years, the airport was closed for over a day and the silence was profound. On this arctic day, I ventured forth on cross-country skis and traversed most of the flatter, upper reaches of the park. Finally, I arrived at the park's former overlook site (no longer there because the trees have grown and obscured the view) and sat on the bench to catch my breath. Comfortably heated from my exertion, I settled into a trance of sorts, my breath melding with the wind.

The rare silence permitted new connections to the land. As when I had been stranded out on the Bush River, I began to sense the Earth's breath as my own. This awareness came, again, accidentally, without intention. The wind swirling around me became a continuation of my body's respiration. The lesson of the shear pin was being replayed – I was sharing my breath and heartbeat with my own place on this quiet February day.

As surely as a person's life can be powerfully affected by a speech, a huge rally, a wedding or a funeral, the energy and circumstance of that silent Winter day washed through my cells and bonded them to my surroundings. Aware of the world at a level just below my consciousness, I became much more tightly bonded to Life as a whole. And just at that moment when I broke through the surface into self-awareness, *the land knew itself through my consciousness.*

Every so often, we need to feel connected to the world around us in this way, to rejoin its rhythms. We need to sense our dependence on the rest of Life, not just dominate it for our own short-run purposes. This sense of reality, of seeing Life the way it is, comes when we have the time and the willingness to place ourselves in the swirling centers of various cycles of Life. These are in short supply in our hurried and overactive world. We need to allow ourselves, and allow our children, opportunities to slow down enough to let the organic wisdom of our place soak into us. Can we free ourselves from packed schedules and the little boxes and layers of comfort where we do not see or experience the richness of Life directly?

When, this time, I was roused from my trance by the cold overtaking the heat of my body, I found myself staring at the Washington Monument standing white against the gray sky. I imagined Martin Luther King, decades earlier, looking out at that very same marble pillar and the sea of people in front of him, stirring souls with his dream. His dream of civil rights brought a new awareness of Human relations to the nation and the world. The dream I had just broken from had stirred me as well and had left me aware of a new relation with my place. The land can move one's soul.

Sound

Some sounds, rather than detracting from our ability to be introspective, actually encourage it. They help us transcend the hurry and fluff of our lives and connect us to the our place. The sonorous tone of a Great-horned Owl is one of these sounds. In the depths of the night, the "whoo-who-whoo, whooo whoo" captures one's attention and settles into recesses of inner thoughts and emotions. Although the owl's call can prompt a shiver, it is not a sound of danger, but one of comfort. Even the silence between the hoots is engrossing, for an awareness of the noble bird lingers. When the plaintive calls finally fade away, one is left refreshed and even a bit awed.

One night, as I sat on my back deck, finishing a late dinner, two Great-horned Owls began calling to each just beyond the edge of the yard. The sound ushered in another story from the past. The hoots of a Great-horned Owl often whisk me back to a night when I was on a camping trip with my 10th grade biology class, as we lay sleeping under the stars beside an abandoned, decrepit sugar mill in Southern Georgia. The looming edifice, silhouetted pine trees and owl sounds were magical. Although I could not see the bird in the dark, I was acutely aware that it could see me. The novelty and mystery of that night long ago brushed my emotions as I sat in the dark behind my house.

We Humans have an innate need to be connected to the world around us. We must eat, drink and breathe the food, water and air of the outside world, that much is obvious. But our need for connection extends far beyond just short-term physical sustenance. We desire the company of other people – friends, mentors, lovers – and we thrive in their presence. After a long, rainy spell, we rejoice in a sunny day and are soothed by the warmth of sunlight on our skin. And sounds – be they music of Human composition or sounds of non-Human nature – can affect us profoundly. Our bodies and minds crave all of these communions and so many more. Scientists are rapidly uncovering evidence of physiological changes with each of these interactions. The presence of friends and loved ones actually changes our body chemistry; it produces a sense of well-being *and* physical health. Exposure to the Sun promotes the production of vitamin D. Sounds are often used to relax or stimulate us – again, producing actual changes in our body chemistry.

These scientific revelations should not come as a surprise. Our bodies and minds tell us directly – with no scientist or textbook as intermediary – of the reality of our many and varied interrelationships with everything around us. In modern culture, however, we are cut off from many of the inputs that our ancestors would have experienced on a daily, seasonal and yearly basis. The temperamental changes in weather, smells of animals and plants, myriad sounds of a diverse biological setting, and even the night sky are alien to many of us today. Since, biologically speaking, we are essentially the same creatures as people two, ten or even hundreds of generations back, how does the loss of these inputs affect us? How do our minds and bodies react now when we are immersed in a very different world than even that of our grandparents?

The swing of seasons, the starry skies, wind in the trees and even the sounds of owls are valuable connections between Humans and the rest of Life, and the loss of our intimate association with them is to our detriment. These associations keep our complex minds occupied in ways they have been for longer than we have *been* Human, and their removal is akin to placing part of our emotions and feelings in solitary confinement. So, as the owl hoots, I crown my raw, emotional response with silent thanks for this rich, wonderful, ancient sound.

Native Voices

I became acquainted with the Donaldsons and Marceys, former denizens of this land, through photographs and historical accounts, relatives of both families, and family heirlooms. The story of this land's *original* Human inhabitants, however, is not so easily grasped. Archaeological studies, books and papers pertaining to local prehistory provide valuable insights, but, one day, while working in the garden, I unearthed a reddish quartzite projectile point that captured my imagination and tugged me in to the story of the Indians who lived here long ago. I turned the fine-grained point over and over in my palm, studying its chipped facets. The sunlight sparkling off the rock inspired me to visit the park's 2,000 year-old Indian encampment site. The site had yielded many similar projectile points (as well as pottery shards and other evidence) when it was excavated, in the 1960s, by Catholic University's Anthropology Department. The site was interpreted to be a seasonal camp used during the Spring and Summer.

The projectile point prompted me to once again take the park's field guide off the shelf. I brought it along to the Donaldson Site to immerse myself in the story of local Indian history. As I read, the quartzite point reminded me of the ties between the ancient peoples of this land to my own experiences here. Vivid images of the past and present once again blended together in my mind.

Indian History of Potomac Overlook

The earliest evidence of Human habitation in Northern Virginia dates to about 11,500 years ago. Archaeologists describe three Native American cultural divisions between this time and the arrival of English colonists at Jamestown in 1607: the Paleoindians (c.9500 -8000 B.C.); the Archaic Indians (c. 8000 – 1300 B.C.); and the Woodland Indians (c. 1300 B.C. - 1607 A.D.). These cultures evolved with climate changes and/or major social and technological developments.

Paleoindians lived in this area near the end of the last ice age. The Chesapeake Bay did not exist at that time, and the Potomac River was entirely non-tidal, flowing fast all the way to the Susquehanna River. The cold, wet climate supported a mosaic of open areas and evergreen and deciduous forests. Groups of Paleoindians moved seasonally to hunt mammals such as bear, deer, elk and perhaps mammoth or mastodon, and to collect edible and otherwise useful plants They used fluted, bi-faced spearpoints (referred to as "Clovis points") for hunting and possibly other tasks.4

One of these Clovis points was found during excavation of a private pool just outside of the park and this fact helps stir the imagination of those attending the Indian History program at the park. After being shown replicas of the Clovis point and the spears to which they were attached, both kids and adults can visualize the small bands of hunters that traversed this very ground thousands of years ago!

To further enliven the experience, park staff demonstrates the use of the atlatl (or spear-thrower) at the field just outside the Nature Center. An atlatl is a weighted piece of wood, about 1 ½ - 3 feet long, that extends the length of the arm and the whipping motion of the wrist. This ancient technology allowed a hunter to hurl a spear two or three times farther and faster than without it. During one particular atlatl demonstration, I faltered and the misguided spear shot high up into a tree 75 yards away! The class and I had a good time speculating whether I could have survived as an ancient hunter. My claims of demonstrating the technique for hunting a now-extinct variety of tree-dwelling bear fell on disbelieving ears and grinning faces.

The appearance of Archaic Indian cultures coincided with the end of the ice age and the resulting climatic changes. As glaciers melted, ocean levels eventually rose some 350 feet. The Chesapeake Bay formed, and the Potomac River became tidal all the way up to the Little Falls area, about a mile and a half upstream from the park. The region became temperate and drier. Hardwood deciduous forests of birch, beech and oak replaced the evergreen and deciduous mosaic. Native American culture changed and adapted with the environment.

Like their predecessors, the Archaic Indians were hunter-gatherers, relying on plants and animals for food. They took advantage of the explosion of living things in the Potomac's newly formed tidewater. Finfish and shellfish were an important part of the Archaic Indians' diet. Archaic Indians moved seasonally in response to fluctuations in their food supplies and occupied the same campsites year after year. One such camp was located just South of Potomac Overlook Regional Park near where Marcey Creek flows over cliffs and into the Potomac.

The shad and herring that constituted part of the Indians' seasonal food supply thousands of years ago still swim from the ocean to spawn at the head of tidal waters of the Potomac. The fish arrive in the river just below the park, splashing and churning by the tens of thousands, in late April and early May. People still gather, just as the Indians did, to harvest some of these fish. Today, most of these fishermen and women are immigrants from Vietnam, El Salvador and other countries. They walk down the steep paths to the river, often with families in tow, to spend the whole day fishing, eating, joking and telling stories. While hiking along the river one afternoon, I came upon a family of El Salvadorans with their spread of food and fishing tackle, and, in my limited Spanish, asked them how the fishing was. Wearing a smile as wide as the river, a young man held up a bucket full of shad that would feed the family for some time.

Within Potomac Overlook Regional Park, an archaeological site known as the "Donaldson Site" provides evidence that Indians continued to live in the area throughout the Early Woodland period (c. 1300 B.C. - 500 B.C.). The Donaldson site is situated high on a ridge, above floodwaters, yet it provides easy access to the Potomac River. Quartz outcroppings and banks of clay provided materials for tools and pottery, and there was plentiful water, including a nearby spring. Fish continued to be an important part of the Woodland Indian diet.

During the archaeological dig, a circle of black residue, twenty feet in diameter, was found at the Donaldson site, and this probably indicated decayed wood from a wigwam. This dwelling would have been made of sapling posts gathered at the top to form a dome shape and tied together with fiber cords and/or vines. The outside was covered with animal skins or bark.

If you are ever tempted to characterize a wigwam or other ancient dwellings as "crude," try building one. Endeavoring to do this with our Junior Naturalist day campers one Summer, we acquired a humble respect for ancient home-builders. From the process of selecting saplings of suitable size and flexibility to the construction of a framework and beyond, we found every step to be as demanding of finely honed skills as most modern construction or carpentry projects. Possessing few of these skills, we ended up with an odd-looking structure that would not have kept us dry or warm through one Summer thunderstorm! Even using store-bought twine and a ladder to join the saplings together, the would-be wigwam ended up lopsided and rickety. The network of grapevines we attached for strength and shape gave the wigwam the look of a ball of yarn after an encounter with a team of playful cats. The bark that we tried to fasten, shingle-like, to the framework, succumbed to the wind and fell off within weeks. It was a sad sight, but it was our first such attempt and gave us an appreciation of the techniques and materials that would have been used to make a livable wigwam two thousand years ago.

The Late Woodland Period (c. 1300 B.C. - 1607 A.D.) in Virginia is marked by the change to agriculture as the primary source of food and, indeed, as the focal point of village life. Villages were located on nutrient-rich bottomland along rivers and streams. Locally, this meant a shift of primary camp and village locations from high areas such as the Donaldson and Marcey Creek sites to low areas such as present day Rosslyn and Roosevelt Island.

At village sites, cultivated fields and houses were interspersed and could cover from two to two hundred acres. Land was cleared for cultivation by bruising trees around the base with stone axes and burning around them to kill the roots. In the planting season, fields were cleared of brush, which was then piled and burned. The topsoil was loosened with a hoe-like tool. Rows of holes, were made with digging stick and into each hole went four grains of corn and two bean seeds. In the spaces between corn and beanstalks the Indians planted squash and sunflowers.

In the Summer of 1608, John Smith and fourteen men set out from Jamestown by boat to explore the Chesapeake Bay and its tributaries. On June 16, 1608, they entered the mouth of the "Patawomeke" River. Smith and his men sailed as far upriver as conditions permitted. They reached a point where they found "mighty rocks growing in some places above the ground as high as the shrubby trees, and various other quarries of different tinctures" Smith's description fits the quarries between Spout Run and

Chain Bridge along the Potomac River (in the vicinity of Potomac Overlook Regional Park). Henry Fleet, a fur trader who sailed up to the Little Falls area soon after Smith, also commented on the abundance of fish and wildlife.

At least once every month or two, I walk over Chain Bridge to enjoy the scenery that Captain Smith saw 400 years ago and to watch for wildlife in the beaver ponds occupying a terrace off the side of the main channel. Often, the main channel is sluggish and low; the cliffs on the Virginia side striated with marks from higher water levels. Occasionally, the water churns high and brown. During the flood of 1996, I was on the bridge just before authorities closed off access to the span. The raging river, barely fifteen feet below the road surface (as opposed to the usual fifty!) made the metal railings hum. Huge tree trunks slammed up against the rock piers. The water extended all the way up to and over the Chesapeake and Ohio Canal, badly damaging its towpath. Six previous Chain Bridges have been washed away by the Potomac. I wondered if this would be the seventh.

Viewing the river during times of normal water levels, I wonder what happens to the wildlife at the beaver ponds during the big floods. The deer can run to safety. Perhaps beaver ride the initial floodwaters down to the wider, quieter tidewater areas and return after the torrent. The wood ducks, night herons and Red-winged Blackbirds simply fly away. The pond-dwelling fish, frogs and other smaller critters are probably swept away from their homes, with no way to return.

Most Native American villages were sited well above the level of the highest floods. The high hills afforded access to the river, yet safety from its vagaries. Rising sea-levels were another problem altogether. Although the Paleoindians were migratory and probably did not have permanent village sites, archaeologists now find their artifacts under the waters of the tidal Potomac and Chesapeake Bay in places that would have been high and dry at the end of the last ice age!

The Historic period was a bleak one for the Indians of Northern Virginia. By 1679 essentially all Indians had been killed (by weapon or disease), driven out of, or had left Northern Virginia, thus ending the Historic Indian period. Governor Spottswood of Virginia concluded a treaty with the Iroquois in 1722 in which they were forced to cede all of the land East of the Appalachian Mountains. This opened all of Virginia for white settlement.

Finishing my reading, I continued to ponder the long story of this Land and its Human inhabitants. The quartzite point I found in the garden held new and renewed meaning, it's source, crafting, and use vivid in my imagination. I made my way back to the house by a longer route past the spring behind the nature center referred to by the Donaldsons as the "Indian Spring." Had an Indian, perchance, crafted the quartzite point in that very location?

West to North

Introspection is an important part of Life increasingly displaced by the rush and race of modern demands. This is a significant loss for quiet contemplation helps bind people, communities and Nature together. Without it, our minds become cluttered with the seemingly endless trivia of the "information age," and we can become confused and overwhelmed. As we take time for introspection, we can absorb what is important and meaningful within the context of a place. Even stories from *other* places and times are absorbed and become part of an organic whole.

The legend of the Zia Sun Symbol is sometimes concluded with the counsel that within Nature, the Human life cycle is the only circle that can become confused; all others turn on their own accord, without thought. To prevent this confusion, older generations must tell the younger generation stories; and the story of Life as a circle is the most important. How much Human misery and suffering is wrought because we do not tell the right stories or have the time to contemplate them? What are the stories that we need to tell?

CHAPTER 3

The North

Strength, endurance and hard work

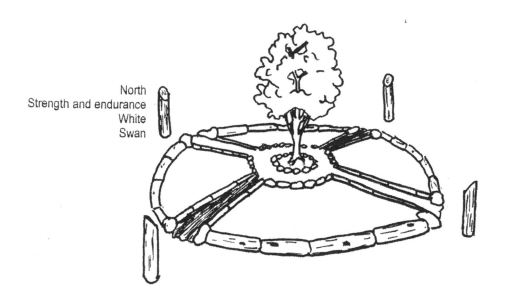

North
Strength and endurance
White
Swan

The Indian Circle Garden has become a focal point for my thoughts. It reminds me of the lessons of the South and the West – that there is a time for nurturing our sense of place and a time for introspection. But it also speaks of the need to occasionally steel ourselves in mind and body; of times we must confront the hardship and even violence that sometimes befall our lives; of times to break a sweat and sing a chant to accompany the body's exertion. These are part of developing our character and bringing out the best in ourselves.

Hardship

One fine November afternoon, I was raking debris out of the Indian Circle Garden and resetting some of the loose log borders. It was a warm day and I took a break from my work, and happened to glance behind me. There, on the ground that I had raked earlier, was a robin, its red breast feathers shining in the afternoon Sun. It stood motionless, looking up at me while I rested. When I returned to work, the robin hopped along in my wake, pecking every so often at the upturned soil. It was hopping down a path of plenty, stuffing itself with worms and grubs. Whenever I stopped and faced the robin, it stopped too, but as soon as I resumed my work, it returned to feeding. After a few minutes of this, the robin flew lazily up towards a nearby walnut tree.

Zing! A brown form shot out from behind the pines at the edge of the garden and bore down upon the robin. It was all a blur, and before I could blink, the Sharp-shinned Hawk, having missed the robin, sped on through to a thicket beyond the orchard. The robin gathered itself, minus a few feathers, and flapped up into the protection of a tangle of vines. There it cried loudly and raised a ruckus with other nearby birds. Just a moment after being on the path of plenty, the robin had found itself on a path of danger and had barely escaped with its life. In the quiet that ensued, I struck a thinker's pose, my palm on the shovel handle and my chin on my knuckles. I stared out toward where the hawk had disappeared.

The four quadrants of the circle garden are delineated by two paths, one running North-South and the other East-West. According to some Indian stories, the North-South path is the good spirit path and the East-West path is the path of trouble and need. These are symbolic of the paths our lives take in reality. According to this story, our lives are most rewarding and meaningful when we travel both paths in balance. An apple tree, planted at the center of the circle where the two paths cross symbolizes a heart in balance and is referred to as the "Tree of Life." Watering and caring for the tree symbolically ensures that we continue to be nourished by the four directions. From the South comes nurturing; from the West, introspection; from the North comes strength and endurance; and, from the East, vision.

I found myself making connections between the symbolism of the circle garden and the predatory event I had just witnessed. The lesson is not simply that times of ease and times of hardship *exist* in life; it may be that we are truly at our best when we experience a mix of the two. Our lives – indeed, our very bodies – are the evolutionary product of those two paths of ease and hardship, and, perhaps because of this, we feel most alive when we experience them both. Robins look and behave the way they do because of the unique blend of ease and hardship that they face. Their senses seek out food and predators with equal acuity, and their form reflects those same factors. The hawk is no different, and Humans, too, are a product of the evolutionary path we have traveled. From our most ancient ancestors to the present day, our bodies and minds have unfolded and flowered in response to the satiation *and* stresses we have encountered. We are truly reflections of the paths of ease and need, good spirit and trouble.

Another connection can be made. The universal story of the circle and the four directions, and others like it, show us that ancient peoples struggled with the meaning of Life just as we do today. They also saw an intimate connection between the meaning of their lives and the elements of Life itself, the rain, the warmth, the air and water. They sensed a need to align their minds in accordance with cycles of Life around them, and recognized that this kind of harmony was not easy to achieve when life was either too difficult or too easy. A central story of the Hopi Indians, for instance, describes their clans' grand migrations to the four corners of the Earth, and their purposeful return to the arid deserts where life was not too easy. It was here at the confluence of ease and hardship that they could fully sense their true connections with Nature and live good, meaningful lives.

Stories, like that of the circle garden, can be misunderstood and misused. It is tempting to believe that following a prescribed ritual can inherently change one's circumstances or well-being. However, circumnavigating the circle garden in some ritualized manner in and of itself will probably not improve our lives in any way. So, do stories actually have value in this scientific age?

In a day when reason seems to rule, we can certainly reason to ourselves that stories and rituals do, indeed, have an enormous role and real effects in our lives. Athletes visualize their skating routines, batting swings and ball releases. Musicians and speakers see their audiences in their minds before they do in real life. These and many other examples are little stories that we tell ourselves to train our physical abilities of muscle control, breath and composure. We raise our children with hundreds of stories, confident in the more-than-superstitious understanding that the stories guide little minds in preparation for real-life situations. Even groups of people, from schools and businesses to entire nations and cultures, derive direction, purpose and cohesion by the stories that they consciously and unconsciously live by. Stories and rituals could be seen as survival adaptations that affect our behavior just above the level of pure instinct, and just below the level of pure reason. By becoming aware of this *through* reason, we can sort out which stories and rituals lead us in sustainable directions and which might lead us down unhealthy paths. Stories and rituals are not all quaint anachronisms – they can lead us to alternate visions of the future. They are, in effect, biological adaptations by which we train our minds. Have we chosen the healthiest stories?

In the past couple of decades, a widespread sustainability movement has emerged to find ways of meeting today's needs without compromising the needs of future generations. This movement has grown both from the grass roots and at high levels of some governments around the globe. Even this modern movement can be informed by ancient stories with timeless relevance. The technologies we invent for providing our energy, food and services are based on the latest scientific discoveries, but if they result in systems that ignore the need to balance the paths of ease and hardship, they will not be sustainable. For most Americans, the most important question for finding the sustainable path may be "how much is enough?" not "how can we produce more?"

American society affords most – but not all – of our citizens with more material comfort than any people ever have had, anywhere on Earth. Money and wealth are not the limiting factors to finding our *collective* way to a sustainable path. Sometimes, they can very well be impediments. When our desire for materials things is borne more out of some intangible need to keep up with or outdo others rather than to fulfill real needs, we can never have enough. Driven, perhaps unconsciously, by stories and rituals that equate happiness with the acquisition of more and more, we lose sight of the fact that there are real limits. While some of us increasingly walk the path of ease and comfort, others find themselves more and more on the path of hardship and pain.

On that same November afternoon that I spent time in the circle garden, I also worked a bit in our compost demonstration area. Composting is one activity that can help fit Human systems into the living systems around us in a sustainable manner. Instead of throwing away leaves, grass clippings and food scraps, we can keep them on the land and recycle them into fertilizer for our yards and gardens. This reduces or eliminates not only energy needed for transporting and processing all of these materials *out* of our lives, but also for producing and transporting fertilizer *in*. It does take work – Human labor – to realize these benefits of composting, but a balance can be struck between the ease and comfort we derive from the food we grow and the work that goes into it. The massive use of fossil fuels for transportation and fertilizers contributes to environmental problems, but it also prevents us from having to do some old-fashioned hard work ourselves. Depending on the level, this is a loss, not a gain!

There are ways to walk the sustainable path, to live happy, contented lives in which we care for our children, our communities, and our world. They are within our grasp if we are willing to search them out and return to an ancient idea that a little hardship is not a bad thing. Compared to the "No Pain, No Gain" mentality espoused at the gyms and spas where we work out, or the tremendous stress we are willing to subject ourselves to with our careers, the hardships of a sustainable world will be a walk in the park. They are simply a different, and more rewarding, set of hardships than the ones we endure now.

Pain

As I walked down the road in front of the Nature Center one day, a noise in the trees overhead caught my attention. Even before I looked up, I unconsciously had deduced that the sound was a gray squirrel leaping through the branches. Nothing new. The arboreal acrobats perform their usual death-defying trapeze acts so commonly that one often tunes them out. This time was different.

The squirrel had leapt from one of the highest branches of a tulip poplar branch, but, on this occasion, did not land safely. Right above me, it scratched and clawed at the leaves of the branch it had intended to reach, but to no avail. The foliage ripped off and the gray rodent began its descent to Earth. I have seen gray squirrels leap from our bird feeders to the concrete fifteen feet below and scurry away as if the impact did not faze them. They spread out their legs and body, making themselves into little parachutes, and land with an acceptable plop. No harm done.

The branch that this particular squirrel had missed, however, was four or five times higher than the feeders. The speed with which the little critter rolled out of its tumble to a parachute-position was remarkable; my cat would have been proud. The squirrel was accelerating, but its fully spread body unable to slow the fall. It only took a second or two, but it seemed like slow motion in my mind. The squirrel hit the pavement with a sickening smack.

Oh, the poor little furry thing! It wasn't dead; perhaps worse, its lower body was paralyzed. It dragged its haunches along in panicked franticness, its front limbs scrambling wildly. As I approached it, the creature responded with a burst of energy by dragging itself off the road and into the edge of the woods. Then, sides heaving, the whites of its eyes showing, it gasped for air and could not move any further. The creature was destined to die a slow, painful death by either its injuries or at the jaws of a predator.

In the face of this intense suffering and fear, I was sick with pity. My reasoning took over only enough to debate putting the tortured squirrel out of its misery. I picked up a large, heavy branch. I approached the squirrel, raised the branch, and was ready to strike the poor creature's head as hard as I could. Adrenalin was flowing and I breathed hard, almost snorting, through my nose.

How marvelous, the will and ability to survive! Life does not want to be extinguished. In all its pain, fear, and suffering, the squirrel scratched and clawed for survival. The thread of desire that connected it with the very beginning of Life tugged hard. It gathered an immense amount of strength one last time and convulsed its entire body. Then, to my amazement, it ran away using all four legs! I stood there with the branch still raised, nostrils flared, still breathing hard, slowly regaining my composure. What possible medical explanation there was for what I had just witnessed still escapes me. I was astounded, and filled with a sense of post-dread – that I had almost snuffed out the life of a creature that somehow defied all odds and lived! The memory of this event further ties me to my place. It is a glimpse into endurance and the will for survival, two of the amazing forces that keep Life going. Life has an affinity for Life.

Years ago, one visitor to the park was a young student whose body was so badly wracked with the deformation of multiple sclerosis that she could hardly keep from sliding out of her wheel chair. And yet she wore a smile and spoke with such excitement and I was overwhelmed with her strength – tough, resilient and compassionate strength. Although the memory of her determined face has faded, her example still inspires me. Confronting hardships far worse than I may ever face, she carried on her life with grace and vibrancy.

Strength, endurance and hard work are all parts of Life. Through testing our limits – intentionally, or when hardship befalls us – we develop character and empathy and better sense our unity with all life around us.

More pain

Anyone who feeds birds, it seems, has a story or two about their attempts to keep squirrels away from the feeders. The intelligence and persistence of these furry rodents is legendary, and most of the stories you hear are true. Working at a park, I have my share of these "shaggy squirrel" stories, and they shed light not only on these amazing creatures, but also on the Humans that do battle with them. The day the squirrel put me in the emergency room, for example, is one of these stories.

Some co-workers and I were having lunch at the Nature Center's library table, and every so often a squirrel would drop from the eaves of the roof onto the platform bird feeder just outside the window. "Hey! Outta there!" one of us would shout. (Sometimes, our exclamations were more colorful, but the squirrels didn't seem to care). Wham! When I gave the window frame a rap, the squirrel would usually go flying off the feeder down into the bushes below. There was no end to them. Like acorns in a windstorm, the rodents dropped from the roof, one after the other, keeping most of the birds away in the process.

After about ten squirrels landed on the platform feeder that lunchtime, I decided to give the next one the scare of its life. I unlatched the window and lay in wait for the victim to drop from the eaves. In the midst of its freefall, I thought, I would knock the window open and send the little bugger flying! So, when the next squirrel dropped, I struck with lightning speed. Glass and blood flew everywhere. I had missed the window frame, hitting the glass instead, and a shard of it sliced my little finger, almost severing the tendon. It was not a pretty sight, and it was off to the emergency room for me!

On emergency room forms there is a line to fill in the cause of the accident. What would you have put? I could think of nothing that would accurately describe the incident *and* save my pride, so I made a truthful accounting. I can still see the doctor's face as he fought to suppress a smile while reading the form. As it turned out, I had a lot of time to ponder my behavior that afternoon. It was a busy day in the ER with many minor injuries like my own and a few cases much more serious. I lay on a table with the curtain drawn, listening to all the commotion. A mere flesh wound on the finger wasn't going to merit attention any time soon.

When I woke up, I was still lying on the table and there was a pool of blood below my hand. I sprang awake and grabbed a gauze pad to press around my finger. As luck would have it, the doctor became available just about then, and he stitched up my tendon and my skin and told me not to be so aggressive toward squirrels. I told him I'd try not to, but within a few days was already plotting the next strategy for keeping the little rodents off the feeder.

A Bit of Relief

The very sources of our pain often bring us relief. Such is the case with squirrels. The endless stories bring laughter to ease any pain they might have caused. Many years ago, we had a sliding glass window at the rear of the nature center with a platform feeder perched just outside, just over the patio. This was another favorite haunt of seed-hungry squirrels. As with the feeder outside the library window, the rodents had access to this feeder from the roof and dropped down to it with ease. Sometimes two or three squirrels assembled on the feeder at the same time, and they seemed to grow fatter and sassier by the day. Sometimes all it took to scare them away was to approach the window, but usually I had to throw open the sliding glass window and utter a couple of choice words.

If squirrels were caught totally unaware, they would often leap from the feeder to the ground below. In the fall, the furry rodents were able to spread their legs and tails out to slow their fall in a manner similar to, but not as effectively as, their flying cousins. Often however, the method of escape was the window screen. When frightened, a squirrel would jump the short distance over to the screen and then run up to the roof. The speed and agility of these animals are simply awe-inspiring!

One morning, I threw the sliding glass window open and a squirrel reflexively leapt for the screen to scurry to the roof. However, neither the little rodent nor I had noticed that the screen was open. The squirrel hurled itself over my shoulder and into the Nature Center, brushing my neck as it shot by. Upon hitting the floor, it went nuts (excuse the phrase, but that's exactly what happened) and completed at least five laps around the main room before I even turned around. The chase was on! I shooed it down the stairs, around the corner into the auditorium, then slammed the door shut behind me. I opened the outside door and then ran back to the other side of the room. From its hiding place behind a potted plant, the bundle of fur saw its opening and dashed outside. After this incident, whenever I saw a squirrel run from me with what seemed undue haste, I wondered if it was one that had sailed over my shoulder.

Swirling Birds

My co-worker, Sarah, and I were taking a morning walk on the trail behind the Nature Center when we witnessed a most unusual and beautiful avian dance. We first heard flittering feathers far over our heads and we both looked up at the same time. Dropping from the canopy of trees high above, were two chickadees swirling in tight, little circles, apparently in an altercation. Perhaps two males fighting over their territories? It *was* breeding season. All during their slow, spiral descent toward us, they were about a foot apart, save for an occasional lunge at each other. As they tussled, their wings fluttered like those of a hummingbird to keep them aloft. We were mesmerized.

It was the appearance of *another* bird made the event especially unique and memorable. Shortly after the two chickadees engaged in their wild spin, a wood thrush materialized as if from thin air. It was also spiraling down toward our disbelieving eyes, making wider, but frantic circles around the two chickadees; a brown and white electron orbiting a black and white nucleus! Sarah and I had no chance to wonder at the oddity of what we witnessed, only time to marvel at it. As the three avian dancers continued their decent, the two chickadees were so preoccupied with their battle they actually hit the ground about a yard away from us! The Wood Thrush pulled out of its dive some distance above terra firma and flew off to some secret place. The chickadees continued scrapping for a second or two and then departed in separate directions.

After the commotion ended, Sarah and I looked at each other with wide eyes as if to say "What in the wide world was *that*??" We could come up with no satisfactory explanation. Perhaps the chickadees were fighting over territory and both of them were, in turn, in the thrush's territory? It was a brief but spirited struggle for something!

Sometimes I recall the curious avian dance as I watch the antics of children as they wait to go on a hike in the woods, stand in line for the bathroom, or otherwise mill about. They enthusiastically buzz about, picking and teasing at each other. Kids on the periphery of any given locus of activity enter the fray as comically as the orbiting thrush. Usually it ends like the story of the swirling birds – a memory with nothing, save an eddy of air, as the outcome. On some occasions, however, teasing becomes taunting and pokes become shoves or punches, and the eddy of air is overpowered by cries, wails, and the brooding energy of hurt feelings.

We are such delicate creatures! Our self-awareness constantly adds to offenses taken and given, our pride often dictates escalation of conflicts far beyond necessity. If the chickadees and the thrush we saw that day had such a burden to bear, they might *still* be pecking at each other, or plotting revenge! We are challenged to show strength and endurance when confronted by our wounded pride or that of others. It is a uniquely Human struggle, carried on for its own sake or to save face rather than simply over whatever it is we want or need. Our ability to tie ourselves back to something larger than ourselves is an aid in this struggle, for it can be a drain for our pride. Surely, this is part of what is meant when we refer to someone as "well-grounded." Like a grounded building protected from lightning strikes, we are better able to dissipate insults and accusations when we are grounded by connections to other people and to the very places that hold and sustain us.

Drought

Every living being must be able to tolerate the ranges of moisture, salinity, nutrients and other necessities that any place offers or it will perish. Some organisms can tolerate wide ranges, some more narrow. The catfish and sunfish that inhabit the fresh waters of the Potomac below the park could not survive in stretches of the river closer to the Chesapeake where the salinity is higher. Shad and herring, on the other hand, journey from the ocean through the brackish waters of the bay and lower river and spawn in the same waters as the catfish and sunfish. Each organism has evolved a set of adaptations that fit the realities of a given place. When those conditions change outside the range of tolerance, organisms must move or die, although some individuals are occasionally suited to survive there. Those that can survive may pass on their traits to their offspring and, over time, a new variety or species arises. There is no intention behind this process, only available ways of living – niches – to be filled.

One Summer I saw the forest struggle with drought. So little rain had fallen that, through my Human perception, the trees and shrubs almost seemed to groan with want of moisture. They pulled their lives along like the proverbial explorer lost in the desert. When a sudden inch of rain punctuated the drought, it was as if the forest had crawled into an oasis and thrown itself at the edge of a tiny pool. The slurping was almost audible.

A few trees died; most began to lose their leaves in August. Silver maples seemed to suffer the most among the trees, spice bush among the shrubs. Would these be the first to disappear from the woods if the climate of our area became drier in the long term? Both seem to require more water than many other trees and shrubs *and* to have a propensity to lose water from their thin leaves. In the floodplain swamps along the Potomac River, where the water table is high, both the spice bush and silver maple were thriving even during the drought.

Humans, too, have adjusted to fit the places we have lived. Before very recent times – when we tapped into huge energy sources that have allowed us to import food, water, and building materials from faraway – our cultures and even our body types reflected the character of our immediate surroundings. Our bodies were reflections of our individual places' rainfall and climate, its soils, the amount of sunlight, and terrain. We were adapted, physically and mentally, to our lands. While this sometimes subjected people to times of hardship and pain – as when drought struck – indigenous people around the world were generally able to cope and to live good, full lives. This is not to romanticize indigenous cultures, for there certainly were and are such peoples that lived difficult, short lives. However, many of the worst examples of terrible plagues, short life-spans and crushing labor, come not from indigenous societies, but from urban areas and the colonies from which these cities got, and still get, resources.

This is not to suggest that, today, we should strive to be like *any* other given society or that we should aspire to ways of indigenous peoples past or present. Modern Western society, largely fed and nourished by resources from faraway places, has certainly enriched us in many ways. However, there are valid questions about how far to take this system. How much is enough? What other factors besides our ease and comfort are part of the equation? What new strategies and economies can our culture adopt in order to promote the appropriate blend of ease and comfort, hardship and struggle? The understanding of place will help reveal the answers to these questions.

Life and Death

The tendency for Human Beings to sometimes consider our own experience the standard by which all is judged and measured is perfectly understandable and sometimes necessary. But such raw anthropomorphism can sometimes prevent us from searching deeply enough – if at all – for wisdom and lessons from Life around us. For instance, based on a rather shallow analysis of Darwin's theory of evolution, our culture has come to think of Life as being defined by brutal competition. Even when, in more recent times, we have come to sense that Life is a balance between competition and cooperation, our Human perspective clouds our understanding. The terms *competition* and *cooperation* carry implicit cultural assumptions of intent that are uniquely Human; they are not part of the non-Human world as such. We can sense the limitations of these words and this mindset when we observe a beehive. At the Nature Center, we keep two or three beehives out back for honey and a glass-encased observation hive inside. Through the glass we witness the intricate lives of our honeybees – birth, death, communication, bounty, starvation, and much more.

Early one morning, I noticed some unusual activity in the display hive. Although most of the bees were clinging to the cells and to each other in quiet torpor, something was astir in a small section of the hive! A few dozen bees, in two or three rows, seemed to be joining forces to keep the queen bee from advancing toward something. As of the day before, however, there had been no queen bee at all! The hive's queen had flown off with about half of the colony a couple of weeks earlier in a population-splitting behavior known as swarming. The queen bee I saw was a *new* queen; she must have emerged during the night!

Why were the worker-bees pushing at the new queen? The next revelation was that a *second* new queen was just beginning to emerge from its pupal cell. Before the second queen could free itself completely, however, the first queen had made it through the phalanx of protective workers and stung it to death. This is the way a hive splits and creates a new queen to ensure its survival. Of the few potential queens that are raised, only one survives. As in cases like I had just witnessed, there is sometimes no contest.

Of course, the fight between potential queens is only possible within the context of the society of bees itself, which is a study of intimate associations between individuals. In our Human terms, we see these associations as *cooperation*, and they could serve us well as models that we intentionally learn from. The individual bees, like cells in a body, are perfectly suited for and *balanced* within the colony. Different duties in the hive are inherited with advancing age – cleaning, ventilation, defense, care of the young and, finally, foraging for food. A system of communication, called the circle dance, enables returning foragers to alert bees in the hive to the direction and distance of food. Complex chemical signals allow for the cohesive actions and responses needed to keep a hive alive. Within this context, there are always varying levels of hardship and pain ranging from drought and disease to the battle of the queens.

The Loss and Rebirth of love

Few forms of pain are more agonizing than the loss of love. Whether it be the breakup of a relationship, the death of a loved one, or the severing of a people from their land, the breaking of heartstrings that tie us passionately to someone or some place can be devastating. Time can heal, but body and emotions can be paralyzed for awhile. These burdens, too, are part of the cyclical character of Life, however, and the stories and rituals we engage determine if and how our pain is transformed. Pain and confusion might linger and our lives might be thrown into further disarray if we delude ourselves with stories that provide an immediate balm, but which are not in accord with reality. The right stories, those that offer visions of how to move beyond the pain and emerge healthier than we were before, sometimes come unbidden.

It was a muggy, warm evening when I returned from California after ending the most binding and passionate relationship I had ever had with a woman. The crickets chirped gently and the dank smell of early September hung in the air, a transition between the humidity of Summer and the crispness of Fall. I entered my house after having been away for six weeks and my cats stared at me as if I had been gone for just a few minutes. Their Summer-shed hair littered the carpet. My heart was ready to crack. The freezing, thawing, and ultimate loss of the precious bond to this woman had hurt me deeply and the pain was unbearable. After dark that night, I wandered around outside, staggered and wounded. I sat down and wept, face buried in my hands, immobilized.

After we parted, I experienced a sense of loss and anguish that I was not prepared for. After a few days, these feelings abated enough for me to carry on everyday life, but sometimes returned suddenly and with debilitating force. But there was also something else . . . a fascination, a sense of something *about* our love that was just out of the grasp of my understanding, just around the corner. About a month after my return, a curious insight came to me as I was driving along an interstate highway. Inexplicably, amid the blur of scenery and the drone of the engine, an image of her lemon tree appeared in my mind.

With the lemon tree came a flood of other images from her home that I could pluck, one by one from my memory like fruit from that tree. Images that gave witness to how closely my ties to *her* were intertwined with her *place*. I thought of her little, white deck perched daintily over the Sacramento River. In one of her first letters, she had enclosed a panorama of three photographs of the river and the deck. During our hours on the phone, she described the scene to me often, wanting intensely to share it with me. She painted pictures in my mind of her street, sheep in her neighbor's yard, her cats . . . and, yes, her lemon tree. When I left, I actually said silent good-byes to the deck, the river, and the lemon tree, and the parting brought tears. The place and the woman I begrudgingly left were burned into my mind and soul; I associated her with the look, smell, feel, and gravity of her place and it with *her*.

She spoke with great love about her home in California. She was born and raised in the Northern-most reach of the vast Central Valley where the valley gives way to the Klamath Mountains, Cascades, and the Sierra Nevada. A warm, dry oasis amid stark beauty. I could feel and sense it. I began to understand her in terms of her land and her land in terms of her. She sent me pictures, talked about her mountains, the sunsets, the valley oaks and digger pines, about Clear Creek. She spoke of when she was young, their family farm, raising sheep, their vegetable garden, shoveling out stalls.

She sent me a map of her town and drew in the landmarks of her life. She gave me a stack of books about hiking the horseshoe of mountains around the town. She created dozens of images in my mind as we talked. I closed my eyes and listened, and her land began to soak into me. It became a part of me even before I ever set foot there. Flying into Redding for first time, I saw the arc of mountains as familiar to me as parts of the Rockies where I had spent much time. The streets of her city were etched in my mind and I drove around a day later with little need for a map.

As I drove up I-95 in Virginia that day, a month after coming home, I suddenly realized that my desire to know her home and her land was part of my desire to know her as a person. And, curiously, my desire to know *her* was part of my desire to know her home. The land had, in fact, captured my imagination years earlier through a book about the mysteries of the Klamath Mountains. Driving and hiking through the

Klamaths, I felt as though I was returning to them, not venturing into them for the first time. Similarly, when I approached her front door for the very first time, and passed her lemon tree, I paused and grasped one of its fruits in my fingers, acknowledging a familiarity that she had created. When we crossed the lawn out to her little white deck, I was overwhelmed with the sense that I had sat on it before and listened to the river.

Oh, it was a mystery. The bond formed between this woman and me had blended imperceptibly with the bond that had formed between me and her place – her land, her home. These ties had somehow been developing in me for years before I ever laid eyes on her. As we explored the rolling hills to the Northeast of Redding, my mind welcomed the park-like oaklands, the gathering evergreens and basalt landscape. When she was away from home for very long, she longed for the look and feel of it. And when I left – even after that first visit – my longing for her had already begun to interweave with a longing for that place. I had visited Northern California a number of times, and each time, I was drawn ever closer to her *and* to that land.

It took some time after my final visit to California for my *own* place to seep back into my pores and veins. Fall brought changing colors, migrating birds, time with my friends, new challenges and a re-establishment of life in my own place. One day I heaved a big sigh of relief for no apparent reason. It untied and expelled a big knot of tension that had gripped my body. Sitting on the bench by the Indian Circle Garden, I suddenly realized that the last vestiges of hurt and anger from the past summer were gone. My heart began to reabsorb the wonders, landmarks, history and stories and people of the land where I lived. I recaptured my sense of place and my place recaptured me, opening my mind once again to the vision it compelled.

North to East

Hardship and pain are inevitable parts of Life. While we can, and should, avoid the extremes, our lives can be enriched when we do not strive to eliminate all troubles or overreact to the hardships that do come our way. Physical labor that tires us, moderation of our appetites and even the welcoming of occasional deprivation are healthy, for in balance with times of ease and comfort, we find the richest and most fulfilling lives.

One irony of modern Human life is that in the quest to avoid hardship, we increasingly and willingly subject ourselves to unprecedented, numbing and often debilitating stresses. The hurried nature of modern life seems to feed on itself and we play willing roles in this acceleration. We find ourselves accumulating material things or undertaking complex plans that were intended to make life easier but which result in more hurry and more stress.

In the United States of the early 21st century, the majority of us do not face *physical* hardships of the nature or severity faced by previous generations, or, by the majority of people in the world today. There are still some in our country who are very wanting for basic necessities and some that suffer from disease, crimes or abuse, but most of us are well fed, well clothed, and well housed. And yet, many Americans, even those that are well taken care of physically, do suffer – from increasing levels of exhaustion and stress, feelings of alienation and from a loss of meaning. Even children are vulnerable to these mental hardships. Is it possible that these conditions stem, at least in part, from our search for the "good life" as we see it portrayed in the media and popular culture? Does our dogged pursuit of physical comforts get in the way of our well-being? Perhaps there are more nourishing visions.

CHAPTER 4

The East

Vision

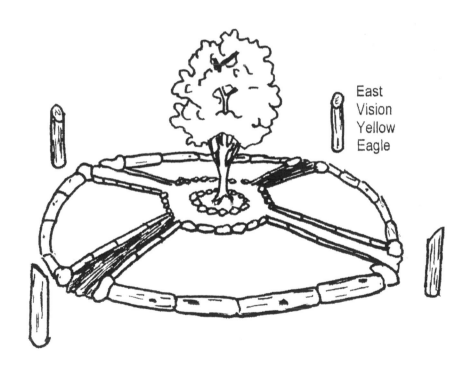

East
Vision
Yellow
Eagle

T he Red-tailed Hawk hung in the wind, its wings pitched at an angle keeping it motionless relative to the ground. Craning our necks to get a better view, we marveled at the bird's aerial balancing act and the reddish hue of its tail, top-lit by the Sun. The hawk made minute compensations for the wind with its alulae – three feathers attached to the index finger of each wing. Then, suddenly agitated, the bird raised a wing and glided off in a wide arc beyond the tree line, calling out "piaaaaaaaaaaah! Piaaaaaaaaaaah!"

After exploring this place through the South, West and North, we now turn to the East – the direction of vision. Many Native Americans revere the hawk and eagle as symbols for vision and illumination – the ability to see into the future, to ensure the wellbeing of the people. Lifted by buoyant air heated by the rising Sun, the birds see not only into the distance, but, symbolically, into time as well.

The modern world, for all of its many benefits and technical wonders, has left us bereft of visions for a sustainable future. We have been guided for over two centuries by the largely unexamined premise that perpetual growth is not only possible, but needed and good. Growth is, indeed, good and needed at some stages of individual lives (Human and other), and in the development of Human societies and ecosystems. However, growth for its own sake is ultimately tangential to the cyclical character of Life and can never be a long-term or continuous proposition. Just as our bodies eventually cease to grow, and just as the seasons mark and symbolize Earth's cycles of growth and decay, so, too, our human institutions are reaching their limits. We are in need of vision.

Despite signs all around us to the contrary, we seem to harbor a curiously unexamined certainty that the growth imperative and the kind of life it drives are our only options. When we do glimpse the need for change, we are easily overwhelmed by a sense of powerlessness and fear at what looks to be an inevitable crash . But it *is* possible for us to soften what will otherwise be a hard fall back to Earth, and the places we live can once again be our inspiration and source of strength. We can transcend our confusion and find ways to reestablish a more healthy equilibrium between our lives and the cycles of Nature.

In the Eye of the Hawk

One of the daily duties of a Potomac Overlook staff member is to feed our captive birds of prey – birds that have been injured, treated by wildlife rehabilitators, and found to be non-releasable. Over the years, we have had an Osprey and a variety of hawks and owls that we feed, care for and occasionally exhibit at educational programs. One, a Red-tail Hawk named "Red," had been shot, and the veterinarian to whom it was taken found it necessary to amputate her right wing. Early in my career at the park, in the midst of the routine task of feeding Red, I unexpectedly tumbled into a new awareness of my connections with Life.

Snow covered the ground on that cold, cloudy afternoon. I shivered as I closed the door to the cage behind me, and Red immediately shifted and ruffled her feathers. In the early days of her captivity, Red was high-strung and would sometimes leap from the perch if my entry into her cage was too sudden. Then she would run, hop and flap around with her stubby right wing throwing her off balance. I'd wait a bit and she'd run back up a branch from the ground to her regular perch.

On this particular day, she remained perched, although I could tell she'd jump in a flash if I moved too quickly. I approached her slowly in order to drop her food – a few mice – onto the feeding platform. The few seconds it took me to end up in front of the beautiful creature now play in slow motion in my memory. I came within an arm's length of her and she sat completely still. I gazed into one of her eyes and it reflected my own in the milky, mid-Winter light. And then, as I stared past my own reflection and deep into the hawk's eye, a most amazing sense befell me. It was as though I were looking through a tiny hole into a huge, glittering and wonderful world beyond, but also knowing that that world was my own. In a way, it was similar to the experience of snorkeling in the ocean – lowering one's goggled face to touch the plane of the water and seeing a shimmering world of fish below, yet feeling the cool breeze on your wet back. This analogy falls short, however, for it was as if my very soul was suddenly linked to that of the bird, and we were separated only by a thin, mysterious film.

I do not know how long I stood there. Seconds, minutes . . . an hour? But it didn't matter, for I have never looked at the world in the same way again. In the eye of the hawk, I had an *emotional* understanding of the absolute unity of all things, all processes, all senses . . . everything. This was no superstitious delusion, but a clarifying, transcendent encounter. It was as real as the cold breezes that blew in my face after I left the cage, and it colored my observation and understanding from that day forward. Just as a seeing the ocean for the first time might attune a landlocked person to the vastness of our planet, what I saw in the hawk's eye sensitized me to the infinite relationships that render our planet not only vast, but essentially alive! I realized that reason and intellect, as powerful as they can be, have their limitations. Alone, they are simply untethered energy, but within the emotional understanding of our relationship to Life, our reason and intellect can be channeled to be of true benefit to individuals and society. What I saw in the eye of the hawk was foundational to the vision that this place inspires in me.

Family Relations

We are a part of a thin, ancient sphere of Life, and our bond to it is basic and seamless. All living beings throughout time are rather like an extended family and the stories of our Human lives blend with the stories of all Life around us. Reminding ourselves of this can enrich even our most ordinary moments and guide us in our everyday actions.

One morning, I came within twenty feet of a deer in the garden without it taking notice of me. There it stood, busily munching a mouthful of morning glory. Oh, did that get my blood boiling! We had worked hard to grow a teepee-shaped trestle of morning glory vines, and now the deer had stripped the bottom four and a half feet of its leaves. As the deer nibbled the heart-shaped leaves – in what seemed to me to be a self-satisfied manner! – the teepee was transformed into a strange and sickly topiary. I had to do something.

As luck would have it, at my feet was a yellow squash. Another garden marauder, most likely a groundhog, had taken a few bites out of it before moving on to another. I picked the damaged squash, broke it into about three or four pieces and tossed one of them at the offending ungulate. The squash arced through the air and struck the deer right on the rump, whereupon the animal leapt into the air and performed a 180-degree turn that would have made a gymnast proud! When it landed, it lurched its head back to its haunches, as if biting at a horsefly. Although it had been looking at me when I hefted the squash, it now took no notice of me. It made no association between the impact of the vegetable on its hind end and the Human Being standing close by. Then it simply went back to chewing morning glory leaves.

Fascination supplanted annoyance. It seemed odd that, after what I had just done, the deer had not raced away into the woods. I took a second piece of squash and lofted it gently so that it would land on the side of animal opposite me. Again, the deer saw my arm move, but paid no attention to the squash flying over its haunches. My aim was perfect, and the chunk landed with a thud about one yard beside the deer. The deer wheeled around, this time without jumping, but with astounding quickness. I had no wish to torment the animal, so after tossing the second piece of squash, I shooed the deer out of the garden and went about my work.

I pondered that incident the rest of the day. This animal was alert to Human presence and ultimately scared off by a yell and a clap, but it did not sense the danger of a flying object, let alone associate it with the animal that it feared. What if it had been a rock or a bullet instead of a mushy piece of squash?

The deer needs to eat, and I need to protect my garden. As long as I am acting with respect towards Life, I feel it is proper to chase and scare the deer. Life has its hardships for both Human and deer, and the deer is nothing if not a creature shaped by the threat of predation. If I lived in an appropriate area – not a park or within a city limit – I might occasionally shoot a deer for my own food; especially if it were eating my vegetables. But I must never 'make a fool of the deer.'[5] By doing so, I would mock myself, for the deer and I are like family in this sphere of Life. I can take what I need, protect what I have and respect what is beyond those boundaries. Knowing when and how to affect Life – even when and how to take it – is an important element of the vision of how life could be.

Beech Drops – A Case of Mistaken Identity

In late Summer, I await the above-ground appearance of purplish-brown sprigs of a plant called beech drops. A diminutive organism with subtle beauty, it emerges only under beech trees. On its thin stalks appear blooms similar to a few other dainty wildflowers such as lobelia and figwort, but otherwise, the plant bears little resemblance to most other flowering plants. For starters, it does not contain chlorophyll and is, therefore, not green at any stage of its life. It is in the Broomrape Family, a group of plants that evolved ways to gain sustenance from *other* plants, and lost the ability to photosynthesize their own food.

The Human response to the path these plants have taken is a fascinating commentary on our understanding of evolution. Consider an account about beech drops from the year 1900:

> *Nearly related to the broom-rape is this less attractive pirate, a taller, brownish-purple plant, with a disagreeable odor, whose erect, branching stem without leaves is still furnished with brownish scales, the remains of what were once green leaves in virtuous*

ancestors, no doubt. But perhaps even these relics of honesty may one day disappear. Nature brands every sinner somehow; and the loss of green from a plant's leaves may be taken as a certain indication that theft of another's food stamps it with this outward and visible sign of guilt. The grains of green to which foliage owes its color are among the most essential of products to honest vegetables that have to grub in the soil for a living, since it is only in such cells as contain it that assimilation of food can take place. As chlorophyll, or leaf-green, acts only under the influence of light and air, most plants expose all the leaf surface possible; but a parasite, which absorbs from others juices already assimilated, certainly has no use for chlorophyll, nor for leaves either; and in the broom-rape, beech-drops, and Indian pipe, among other thieves, we see leaves degenerated into bracts more or less without color, according to the extent of their crime. Now they cannot manufacture carbohydrates, even if they would, any more than a fungi can.6

Is beech drops a *thief*. . .a dishonest member of the plant kingdom? Is it possible for plants to be such things? To some, these words, from a century ago, might appear misguided or quaint, but even if such prose rarely appears in the 21st century, a similar sentiment still abounds. It is still a common view that various parts of Nature have *purposes* as though they were created, ready-made, for fitting into a statically operating machine. When Nature is thus perceived, organisms such as beech drops are sometimes deemed to have *lost their purpose*. Thus, the retiring beech drops, having descended from plants that at one time had chlorophyll for photosynthesis, is sometimes considered, even today, to be an anomaly: an outcast in the grand design of Life.

And, yet, Nature changes constantly and individual species – including beech drops – are part of this adaptation. Through the eons,

Nature evolves as a whole, living system. Very few organisms have remained the same over geologic spans of time, and those that do are referred to as "living fossils." Beech drops is simply a plant that *has* changed and now occupies an available niche that another organism had not yet occupied.

Another common notion about Nature competes with the static view just described – that of *progress* in evolution. This view allows for a changing and evolving system, but sees it as advancing, inexorably, in one direction. Human Beings are considered the pinnacle of evolution, more advanced in the hierarchy of Life. An organism such as beech drops is thus seen as a hapless character of sorts, mired in a backwater eddy off the main stream of evolution.

This view, too, is not consistent with a study of our Earth's past nor with an in-depth knowledge of place. The geologic record reveals that evolution is more like a dance than a stream, and that organisms, themselves, have been changing in no direction other than that which affords survival of both themselves and the living systems of which they are a part. The trends of larger brains and more efficient metabolism are more an artifact of the reality that from a very simple beginning, there have been seemingly infinite paths of complexity for evolutionary change to follow. However, whether because limits were reached or that alternate paths were advantageous (as in the case of beech drops), evolution has often taken what seems to be *steps backward*. Whales and seals evolved from land mammals that themselves had crawled *out* of the ocean eons before. The so-called "advanced salamanders" do not have lungs, but evolved from those that did. And plants like beech drops lost the ability to photosynthesize as they acquired other metabolic pathways to sustain themselves – pathways that were tied in with the metabolic products of the beech trees. There may be no inherent "directionality" to how organisms evolve other than the myriad (but limited) niches that are available to be filled.

By transcending the anthropomorphic values inherent in the two views of Nature described above, beech drops suddenly becomes a much more fascinating plant! This herbaceous annual has root-like structures called haustoria that grow into the roots of beech trees and absorb the small amount of nutrients necessary to sustain its underground growth and its modest flower stalk in the Fall. Though it is sometimes considered a parasite, it would be a mistake to assume that beech drops is harmful to the beech tree. Despite the fact that the little broomrapes are found under almost every beech tree in the park, the trees are common and healthy. More likely, there is a mutualistic relationship between the herb and the tree in which each gains sustenance from the activity of the other. It is possible that the roots of beech drops, like the hyphae of fungi, might actually help beech trees absorb certain nutrients that they would be less able to on their own. Or, perhaps, the underground growth of beech drops provides a network of organic matter that helps prevent soil erosion.

In the absence of evidence that beech drops actually *harms* beech trees, it is safer to assume that the two provide sustenance for each other just like bacteria in our intestines are indispensable to our digestion. Perhaps this is what Thoreau meant when he noted the fact that the roots of broomrapes grew in the roots of other plants and observed that "There are minds which so have their roots in other minds as in the womb of nature – if, indeed, most are not such?!" Thoreau seemed to understand that all parts of Life are so interconnected with each other that they are essentially a single entity.

Science now corroborates this associative character of Life – Nature is not fundamentally "red in tooth and claw," but only honed at the edges by this competition. Nature's foundation is one of associations among organisms and between organisms and the entire system of Life. If we Humans adopt this view and use it intentionally, we refer to it as cooperation. Seeing Human Beings as *part* of a vast network of Life and not its destined end product is an element of the vision that can flow from any place.

The Limits of Nature

Summertime in the mid-Atlantic is an amazing time of growth. Lawns grow rampant, vines sprawl everywhere, forest canopies blot out the Sun; we are overwhelmed with greenery. One hot, steamy Virginia day, I asked myself: "Why isn't Antarctica covered with trees?" For that matter, "Why doesn't the Sahara hum with life?" or "why are animals and plants not found in abundance on Himalayan peaks?" At first, the answers to these questions seem self-evident: "It's too cold, or too dry, or there is not enough oxygen!" Consider, however, that Nature has had billions of years to experiment with new forms of Life. Why hasn't she given birth to all sorts of plants and animals to clothe Antarctica, the Sahara and the Himalayas as densely as forest in the Eastern U. S. and elsewhere? It seems odd that the endless evolution of Life on this planet has not resulted in an abundance of organisms that can thrive in very cold, dry or oxygen-poor places.

A second look reveals that it is not odd at all. There are, indeed, absolute limits that cannot be overcome even by Mother Nature and Father Time. This notion of absolute limits is uncomfortable to some, but since we are a part of Nature – not apart from her – we are subject to those limits. Limits exist even in seemingly plentiful environments. The furious growth in our lush forests and our gardens soon levels off and enters a state of equilibrium. Winter brings a time of recession, followed by renewed growth in the Spring. These limits and cycles are as inherent as gravity, and we are often reminded of them if we carefully observe the places we live.

If there are limits, then there are ways to approach those limits in a healthy manner, or to stay away from them altogether. A clue to how Nature accomplishes this can be seen in the ways living things grow.

In healthy organisms, hormones and enzymes that stimulate growth are always counteracted by growth inhibitors. Even more to the point, the direction and character of an organism's growth are governed more by growth *inhibitors* than by growth *stimulators*. A healthy organism always moderates its own growth and, in most cases, stops growing at a predetermined level.

One can see this everywhere in Nature. The oaks, foxes and even the rampant porcelain-berry vines grow in precise and measured ways that one can see and understand. What happens at the molecular level shows us why and how this is.

The plant hormone, abscisic acid, provides an example of this universal phenomenon of growth moderation. Abscisic acid shuts down the production of proteins and thus slows growth in plants. The hormone is produced in the tips of roots (among other places) and is transported up the roots toward the shoot. If a root that normally grows straight down (a taproot, for instance) is, in fact, growing in that direction, abscisic acid is distributed to the entire root and moderates growth evenly. If, however, the root starts to grow horizontally because of an obstruction in the soil or some other reason, the hormone is concentrated on the lower side of the root. This slows growth on the lower side relative to the upper side and the root again turns downward. An alternative way for a root to turn downward would be for growth to be *stimulated* on the upper part. However, this system would result in unchecked growth, the outstripping of available resources such as water and nutrients and, ultimately, the death of the plant. Like a car without brakes careening down a hill, swerving faster and faster from one side of the road to the other, this unchecked growth would be out of control. In fact, some herbicides work by preventing growth inhibition in plants! Uncontrolled growth is lethal. I sprayed a dandelion with such a herbicide and watched it twist and turn and grow to twice its normal size in one day and then collapse dead on the second day.

The moderation and occasional cessation of growth are rules in Nature with very few exceptions. Sometimes growth is checked from the outside, as when food shortages result in starvation or lower fertility, but often it is checked by an internal mechanism. Abscisic acid and other growth moderators are adaptations just as surely as a bee's wing or a fox's tooth, and they allow organisms to be sustained within the set of real limits and prevent the catastrophic breaching of those limits. We Humans have the ability to anticipate the future and even change our behavior. Do we have the capacity to limit our growth?

Perhaps the most important limiting factor to growth of all systems – including Human systems – is energy availability. People were able to expand their populations into Northerly climes hundreds of thousands of years ago after the discovery of fire. The development of agriculture provided the food energy that sparked a steady rise in Human populations. The Native Americans of the Chesapeake Bay region were just beginning to climb to these population plateaus when their European conquerors – who had already reached such populations in their own homelands – arrived here in the 1600's. The harnessing of fossil fuels two hundred years ago enabled exponential growth in both Human population and material transformation and consumption.

In recent years, Human energy use has become a critical issue. Our culture, which has produced so many wonderful advances for Human life, has also grown explosively – in population and in consumption of energy and materials – without much inhibition. Recent generations have come to believe that growth is good in and of itself – even a fact of Life. Many of us fear limits and the cessation of growth. Instead of adjusting our activities to approach these limits in healthy ways or to steer clear of them, we clamor for more.

The conventional wisdom, which assumes few or no limits, now encourages us to pursue the "perfect" energy source – one that is cheap, plentiful and even pollution-free. We are promised clean-coal technology, fuel cells that produce nothing but water vapor as exhaust, and even nuclear power with perfect containment of waste products. However, even if these new systems were to be perfectly (and miraculously!) pollution-free, they will ultimately be harmful to us if we do not grasp the reality of limits. I consider this as I pluck the dandelion that suffered its undignified demise from a lack of inhibitions.

When I observe how Nature works in my place, I see an intricately interwoven and interrelated set of organisms and processes that are subject to the same principles of limits that govern Nature as a whole. The reality of limits and the need for Humans to honor – and even celebrate them – entwines itself into my vision.

The Pace of Nature

Viewing our work and leisure as Human enterprises only and not as emanations of Nature's cycles of days, months and seasons, yields very strange and distressing developments. Our work – even if it is hardship and toil – can become the only way we enjoy ourselves, while opportunities for ease and comfort can cause feelings of restlessness and guilt. This ironic state of affairs results from our ideas of time and progress. It is not that we do not *desire* ease and comfort – our seemingly insatiable urge to acquire toys and time-saving devices belies that notion. When it comes to taking the time necessary to rest, recreate and to enjoy the fruits of our labors, however, we are often reluctant or confused.

When I venture out of the park and into the city that surrounds me, I am immediately swept up in the modern Human time scale that buffets our more ancient rhythms . Honking horns, hyper-scheduled days, the constant message of "buy, buy, buy!" and other such hurries and worries invade my consciousness. For better or worse, it is very possible to acclimatize to this alternative time scale, and some people even feel as if they thrive in it. The modern way of ordering our lives around time is not the *only* way, however, and when we begin to examine our underlying assumptions, new visions can emerge.

Consider the joke about a city-slicker who was driving down a rural road on his way to a meeting when he happened by a certain farm. As he drove by the house in the early afternoon, he saw the farmer sitting on the porch smoking a pipe. The city-slicker was amazed and a little indignant that the farmer should be lazing there with so many hours left in the day. He drove up near the porch and asked "The day is so young, Mr. farmer; don't you have any work that needs to be done?"

The farmer drawled, "Well, I got my planting and hoeing done for the day, so I reckoned I'd just a sit here and have a smoke. You lost?"

"No, I'm not lost!" the city-slicker blustered as he dropped his cell phone. "Surely there must be something you could be doing to increase your cash-flow, or perhaps you could make some investments."

"Why would I want to increase my cash flow or make investments?" queried the farmer, between puffs.

"Well, then you could put away your earnings in a nice big fat bank account" came the answer.

"Why would I need a big fat bank account?"

A bit exasperated, the city-slicker blurted out "Isn't it obvious? If you had a big fat bank account, you could retire early, and then you could enjoy yourself and do whatever you wanted!"

"I'm doing exactly what I want to be doing right now, and was enjoying it just fine until you came driving up with all these silly questions! You sure you ain't lost?"

One of the deepest and most profound ways we make sense of the world is through our perception of time. The awareness of self, and of time and the future may be among the first characteristics that set our early ancestors apart as truly Human. Our *modern* ideas about time are so firmly embedded that they can easily be taken for granted. And yet, Human Beings have had many widely differing concepts about time that vary with culture, point in history, and individuals. Just as Einstein challenged modern Western assumptions about time, so too would other world-views. Our assumptions about time affect our day-to-day life more than most anything else.

An exploration into assumptions about time is essentially an exploration of the relationship between Human nature and Nature as a whole. Whether it be solar or lunar time (from which come our calendars and daily schedules), atomic time, or other standards, time is essentially measured by changes that happen in Nature. After Human Beings evolved the ability to be consciously aware of these changes – and therefore aware of what time was – we quickly formed mental grooves that were useful to explain and deal with time's consequences (such as aging, death, and the mystery of what happens after death). These grooves have usually served well the various cultures that invented them, but they have occasionally changed or evolved. In today's hurried world, where time-saving devices yield less spare time than ever, where "time is money," and where people always seem to be in a race against the clock, we could benefit from an examination of our assumptions.

What are some of the different ways of thinking about time? There are at least two (and probably three) broad views on the subject. The first of these might be called "circular time." This view of time is based on early Humanity's observations about the cyclical patterns of Nature. Since seasons, months and days were cyclical, just like life cycles, water cycles, and other cycles in Nature, most peoples around the world patterned their activities accordingly. Jeremy Rifkin noted in his book Time Wars[7] that "earlier peoples had made little or no distinction between past, present, and future, preferring to experience reality as an ever-recurring state of existence. The cyclical sense of time mirrored the ecological and astronomical cycles, bonding human consciousness and culture to the rhythms of Nature." I think often of these words when I think of past

Human inhabitants of my place. How did they view time? Did they ever feel *hurried* in the modern sense of the word?

This feeling of being in synchrony with the cycles of Nature is largely gone in modern society, but we all taste it occasionally. Sometimes when we are taking a walk on a beautiful day, sitting engrossed with a good book, or in the company of a friend or mate, we get lost in the moment and lose track of time. In <u>Walden,</u> Thoreau wrote tantalizingly about being so engrossed with one's surroundings that time drops away.

> *Sometimes, on a summer morning, having taken my accustomed bath, I sat in my sunny doorway from sunrise till noon, rapt in a reverie, amidst the pines and hickories and sumachs, in undisturbed solitude and stillness, while the birds sang around or flitted noiselessly through the house, until by the sunlight falling in at my West window, or the noise of some traveler's wagon on the distant highway, I was reminded of the lapse of time. I grew in those seasons, like corn in the night, and they were far better than any work of the hands would have been. They were not time subtracted from my life, but so much over and above my usual allowance . . . For the most part, I minded not how the hours went. The day advanced as if to light some work of mine; it was morning, and lo, now it is evening, and nothing memorable is accomplished. . . . My days were not days of the week, bearing the stamp of any heathen deity, nor were they minced into hours and fretted by the ticking of the clock; for I lived like the Puri Indians, of whom it is said that for yesterday, today, and tomorrow they have only one word, and they express the variety of meaning by pointing backward for yesterday, forward for tomorrow, and overhead for the passing day. This was sheer idleness to my fellow townsmen, no doubt; but if the birds and flowers had tried me by their standard, I should not have been found wanting. A man must find his occasion in himself, it*

is true. The natural day is very calm, and will hardly reprove his indolence.8

As with Thoreau's fellow townsmen, we, too, find it difficult to understand Thoreau's "natural day." We move at a different pace and to a different beat than older cultures. Even more to the point, however, is that our deepest conception of time has become linear due to a number of philosophical departures from the older, circular stories and experience of life. The scientific viewpoint that has dominated our culture for half a millennium has instilled in us a deeply ingrained story of time. Despite the fact that more recent science has shattered old assumptions about time, popular understanding has yet to catch up.

Hundreds of years ago, Renaissance scientists began comparing Nature to a finely crafted clock, which, once started, was ticking along indefinitely. The intense awareness of the cyclicity of Nature began to fade in the face of the observation that nothing is ever exactly as it was. From this grew a more linear conception of time in which Humans and all of Nature journeyed along a path with a definite starting point and endpoint. The comfort afforded the Human mind by the continual return to familiar starting points of days, seasons, and other cycles was overshadowed by a daunting journey into an unknown future. To cope with and justify this new linear approach to time, we had to imbue it with goodness and validity. Since time was now linear, each successive moment had to be better than the previous one for life to make sense. With a linear concept of time, one could only be happy in the Spring of one year if it was *measurably better* than the Spring of the previous year. The comfort of the return was shattered.

The assumption of linear time colors our thoughts on just about everything. It underlies our ideas of progress, economic growth, personal growth, and even good and bad. Even the theory of evolution is commonly viewed as Life progressing along the path of time, and we see our own species as the best and *most evolved*.

How does this kind of thinking affect us? To be sure, certain exciting and interesting insights and experiences have been gained with a linear point of view. It can create a milieu of constant challenge that, for some, is intoxicating. But there is a dark side as well. Although Darwin himself did not equate evolution with progress, others fit his findings quite nicely into their own linear worldviews. Industrialists of the late 1800's coined the term "social Darwinism," and used the budding interest in evolution to justify the vast injustices of the industrial revolution. In Darwin's <u>My Several Publications</u>, we see that the scientist, himself, struggled with a restlessness and inability to enjoy the moment that he lamented.

> *I have said that in one respect my mind has changed during the last twenty or thirty years. Up to the age of thirty, or beyond it, poetry of many kinds . . . gave me great pleasure, and even as a schoolboy, I took intense delight in Shakespeare . . . I have also said that formerly pictures gave me considerable, and music very great delight. But now for many years I cannot endure to read a line of poetry: I have tried lately to read Shakespeare, and found it so intolerably dull that it nauseated me. I have also almost lost my taste for pictures or music."*

Darwin saw his loss of ability to enjoy literature and the arts as a serious shortcoming and mused that brain atrophy or his mental constitution may have been responsible. He concluded that "The loss of these tastes is a loss of happiness, and may possibly be injurious to the intellect, and more probably to the moral character, by enfeebling the emotional part of our nature."[9]

These words strike close to home. They reflect and presage our inability to slow down enough to enjoy not only poetry, music and art, but also the company of friends and family, an interesting trip, or even time when we "do" nothing. We are often so concerned with preparing for a bigger and better future that we find it ever harder to enjoy the present.

It is ironic that societies with the most time-saving devices are often the most hurried and harried. This apparent contradiction is explained when one realizes that most "time-saving devices" are not really that at all, but instead are "production-increasing devices." With our linear way of thinking, we use our inventions to produce more but not to save time. When we *do* save time, we are often at a loss as to what to do with it other than to produce something else! We are caught in the city-slicker's vicious circle and find it difficult to relax on the porch like the farmer. Time, and our relationship to it, is a profoundly basic part of Human existence. Although we are creatures who can abstractly sense the past and future and create mental constructs of time, we often don't see that time is a phenomenon of Nature as a whole. This realization is difficult to grasp unless we are rooted in one place and thus able to see ourselves as part of Nature. The ability to understand our lives within the context of Nature's rhythms is an important part of a new vision.

A Brand New Ancient View of Life

Over the years, the lens of my experience and learning through which I view the world has evolved, and, so too, the understanding of my place. As I go on walks through the woods, I see Life differently than when I first arrived in this place almost three decades ago. My perception is crowded with the faces of Life around me, the ideas that have come my way; the contemplation of my past and with Life itself. Park visitors, former inhabitants of this land, foxes, butterflies, bacteria and fungi, the bedrock of mica schist, the Sun's energy and the power of wind and snowstorms coalesce in the vision of absolute unity that I sensed in the eye of the hawk.

After having lived in this forest for several years, I suddenly was impressed, one day, by what seemed to be a counterintuitive pattern of fallen logs on a hillside. If I had been asked to predict, sight unseen, which way trees would have tipped over on the steep slope, I would have said, "downhill – in the direction of the slope." Instead, it appeared that very few logs were situated this way. In fact, a surprising percentage of them were oriented perpendicularly to the hill, having fallen sideways with apparent indifference to gravity. It was an almost terraced hillside on which leaves, debris, and, ultimately, soil collected on the up-slope side of the toppled trees. The effect of this pattern was that soil was built up faster and erosion occurred more slowly than would have been the case if all the trees had fallen nearly straight downhill.

"How could this be?" I wondered to myself. It was not just that the trees were falling in a direction that was different than one would expect. They were also falling in a way that promoted maintenance of the soil so necessary for the healthy growth of future trees and other plants as well! It wasn't long before I had an idea. Trees growing on hillsides buttress themselves to counter the effects of gravity; the lower parts of their trunks flare to the uphill and downhill sides to provide a support against the pull of gravity. (That trees can sense and respond to gravity is easily seen when a tree that is knocked over grows new shoots straight up.) The buttressed bases profoundly influence the direction in which the trees will tip when old and rotten or when knocked over by wind or the impact of another tree. They are more likely to fall sideways because that is the direction of least resistance.

Could the trees *know* that it is to their benefit to fall sideways? Of course not; at least not in a conscious manner. But it certainly seems to work out just as beneficially for them as if they did. Perhaps in addition to the structural advantage trees gained through the evolution of growing buttressed trunks, other advantages were gained through a long-term process of genetic selection such as the maintenance of their own soil! Perhaps the buttressing is more pronounced than is necessary simply to hold the tree up against gravity, thus resulting in a higher percentage of trees that fall sideways. These are testable hypotheses.

These new insights and questions were outgrowths of a grand and overarching way of looking at Life that had alternately nudged and been nudged by my existing worldview over a period of many years. The manner in which I viewed the world blended with the daily reality of my place *and* with the insights of an elderly English scientist and inventor, James Lovelock, whose story is changing the world.

During the 1970s, Lovelock strolled the English countryside with his neighbor, William Golding, the famous poet and author of Lord of the Flies. Lovelock told Golding about his newly crystallizing views of how the atmosphere of Earth was explicable in the context of Life, of how different it is from those of Mars and Venus. In his soft, yet animated, way he spoke of how it seemed that organic and inorganic parts of Earth (rocks, water, air) had evolved together to form a tightly coupled living system that was self-generating and self-regulating. The entire planet's surface was alive now, or had been changed by Life. The chalk downs that were part of Golding's and Lovelock's place were, after all, the remains of seashells of ancient oceans. Lovelock told Golding that the Earth behaved as if it were a single living entity – a superorganism.

Upon considering these ideas, Golding suggested something that would have profound implications for science and society. In response to Lovelock's need for a name to characterize the homeostatic system he was describing, Golding suggested "Gaia" after the ancient Greek Goddess of Earth. After all, people thousands of years ago thought the Earth to be alive, and now science was rediscovering this important worldview.

Like most new ideas – especially grand, sweeping theories such as evolution and plate tectonics before it – Gaia Hypothesis was mostly ignored for many years.

Whenever mentioned by evolutionary biologists, it was ridiculed. Lovelock had taken an unusual step when he named the theory "Gaia" instead of a more technical appellation. To many scientists, the title, Gaia, connoted mysticism and they distanced themselves from the idea more than they might have if Lovelock had chosen a name such as geophysiology, or Earth system science. Others took issue with Lovelock's claims that the superorganism of Earth had been self-generated and was now self-regulating, or they criticized the lack of demonstrated mechanisms by which Gaia could exist.

Relatively quickly, however, Lovelock's research yielded compelling new evidence in support of the Gaia Hypothesis. He showed that the Gaian system regulated atmospheric gasses that react with living beings – oxygen, methane, carbon dioxide, hydrogen sulfide – about forty, in all. The maintenance of oxygen at around 20% in the atmosphere for hundreds of million years is an example. Ocean alkalinity, air temperature and other environmental factors have been shown to be heavily influenced – if not regulated – by Life. Lovelock and his colleagues explored ways in which the climate and the global sulfur cycle might be moderated by microorganisms in the ocean that release gasses that influence cloud formation. Myriad processes such as feeding, excretion, breathing, reproduction, lightning, water condensation, and untold others dance together in the Gaian system.

Even though the Sun has increased its radiance (and thereby, its potential to heat the Earth) by almost a third during the time span of Life on this planet, the living system that Lovelock described has maintained temperatures within a fairly narrow range suitable for its own existence. These thoughts were dancing around in my head as I sat in a lawn chair one day enjoying the early Summer Sun and an article about Lovelock. As I glanced up from my reading, my attention was suddenly riveted on a potato leaf growing beside me in the garden. It was an incredibly vibrant and deep green. The bright sunlight and the slight breeze cast their energy on the leaf making it throb with vitality!

My place is defined by the color green for seven months of each year; the other five months live largely from the fruits of the seven. The light of the Sun is reflected back to our eyes as green because the other colors are absorbed in leaves and trigger the wonderful, glorious process of photosynthesis. Using the energy of the Sun's light, plants assemble carbon dioxide and water – low-energy molecules – into high-energy sugars and give off oxygen in the process. These photosynthesized sugars provide the fuel that turns the Circle of Life. The primacy of photosynthesis sunk itself to my core that afternoon, and the significance of East as the direction of Vision took on added meaning. East, the direction of the rising Sun, illuminates our path, showing us where and how to proceed.

The deep green of the potato leaf was incredibly beautiful to me, as well it should have been. The greenness of Nature is a reflection of the very foundations and longevity of Life on this planet. *Invented* by the ancestors of blue-green bacteria about 3 billion years ago, photosynthesis was the process that truly made Life a circle! At that time, many sizes and kinds of bacteria were our planet's only forms of Life. Small varieties consumed high-energy molecules that were a part of the so-called "primordial soup" – the ultimate energy source at that time. Certain bacteria ate the remains of other bacteria, and most bacteria ate the wastes of others. Eventually, however, this resulted in a net production of waste products that were simple molecules with little embodied energy. As it may have on Mars, Life could have easily come to a grinding halt on Earth.

Happily, organisms adapted in at least two ways that solved this dilemma and allowed Life to continue. First, bacteria evolved the ability to photosynthesize – to use sunlight to re-energize the low-energy molecules around them and turn them into food and useful energy. Purple photosynthesizing bacteria were the first to do this, using carbon dioxide and hydrogen or hydrogen sulfide as the raw materials for their bodies and energy for their activities. Subsequently, blue-green bacteria developed a more productive photosynthesis that used water in place of less common hydrogen molecules.

Second, when some larger organisms ingested blue-green bacteria instead of breaking them down for food, which would result in more low-energy molecules, they evolved permanent interactive, physical partnerships with them. The chloroplasts (the solar energy-using packets) of plants all around us are the evolutionary remnants of free-living, photosynthetic bacteria that formed seamless symbiotic ventures with other organisms!

These realities of evolution were rediscovered in the 1970's by Lynn Margulis, formerly the Distinguished University Professor in the Department of Geosciences at the University of Massachusetts. With overwhelming evidence, her "endosymbios theory of cell evolution" was reluctantly, but eventually, accepted by scientists in the 1970s and 1980s and showed that there was much more to evolution than Darwin knew, or could have known. Darwin could not study in detail or appreciate the importance of microorganisms - the building blocks of all Life and its evolution. Physiologic behavior and community activities of microbes enmeshed the metabolism of different kinds of organisms and allowed Life to flourish billions of years ago, and *became the foundation for all subsequent larger forms of Life*. In her book, *Symbiotic Planet*, Margulis observed that people are generally unaware of the prevalence of symbiosis. She notes that "if you look at your backyard or community park, symbionts are not obvious, but they are omnipresent."[10]

Albeit from a very different perspective, Lynn Margulis' research led her to many of the same conclusions as James Lovelock and she became an enthusiastic supporter of the Gaia Hypothesis. She collected information about microbes, their behaviors, community ecology and physiologic interactions that underlay the understanding of how Life controls many aspects of its environment and ultimately affects Planet Earth's climate, ocean salinity and atmospheric content. One of the ways in which this happens is through carbon burial. Over the eons, living organisms incorporated carbon dioxide – the gaseous form that carbon takes in the atmosphere – into solid rock such as limestone (calcium carbonate) and coal (largely carbon) and other fossil fuels. With large amounts of carbon thus buried and sequestered away from reacting with oxygen, carbon dioxide levels began to decrease rapidly from about 95% of atmospheric gas when Life began to the 0.03% it is today. As it happens, carbon dioxide is also one of the most effective greenhouse gasses (gases that trap heat in the atmosphere and slow its escape to space). Despite the fact that the Sun is about one third brighter now than it was when Life began, our thinning blanket of carbon dioxide allows for the maintenance of temperatures suitable for Life. Just as the buttressed trees on the hillsides seem to affect more than just structural integrity, the Living processes that transferred carbon from the atmosphere to coal swamps and limestone had significance far beyond their short-term effect.

The Gaia Hypothesis began to be known as Gaia Theory in the 1990s due both to its increasing acceptance and the fact that Lovelock argued that it could now be used to generate its own hypotheses and accurately predict their outcomes. Gaia Theory now hovers at the brink of mainstream science – especially when it is euphemistically referred to as "Earth System Science." Although the breadth and scope of the theory make it difficult for everyone to agree on all its facets, many scientists fully support the general idea and others speak of its tremendous potential as a model for inquiry. When we look at pictures of our beautiful planet taken from outer space, a new and powerful story starts to unfold. Life is not simply isolated organisms on the "third rock from the Sun," but is understood as a self-regulating system comprising the entire surface of Earth. This story, too, has blended with my place and has become part of the vision.

NASA Image

Prelude to a Vision

I came to sit again at the bench near the Indian Circle Garden. The Sun was a big, fiery ball in the East. A cool morning breeze comforted my body and freed my mind to wander and roam over the landscape. As I sat in contemplative silence, previously unrelated strands of Life began to weave themselves into a vision. A few of those strands seemed dominant in the tapestry, and one of these was time. Through the lens of my place, I can see a time when Human life will proceed at a slower pace. Many thrilling and exciting experiences will be embedded in our lives and we will move and think fast when we need to, but superfluous hurry will be an anomaly, not the norm. The life of a hawk, largely spent perched or soaring in great circles, is punctuated with fantastic dives and other moments of high drama. And how much *more* drama is inevitably a part of a Human life, whether at rest or in action, than that of a bird of prey! How well provided we are for living interesting, challenging and fulfilling lives!

I can see us collectively taking a deep breath and releasing a sigh as we abandon many of the activities of our frenetic world. It is very possible, especially as we come to see that the supposed benefits of all this hurry are unmet. So much of what we do now results in the unfettered depletion of Earth's living system *and* of our own time and energy. Our culture is beginning to examine and challenge the prevailing growth-for-growth's-sake economy, but many years from now we may look back and wonder how we went so long before doing so. We may marvel at how driven we were to maintain this growth-based economy – often at the expense of our wellbeing!

We are bombarded from all sides by advertisements and other messages designed to trigger dissatisfaction so that we, who have so much material wealth already, might desire and purchase even more. We can forgive ourselves for falling into this trap, for the messages are powerful. But, when we recognize what is happening, we actually begin to become dissatisfied at being prodded into dissatisfaction! We can then examine the idea of what is *enough* and find renewed contentment in the richness of our places at a slower pace. The disciplined reconnection to a place offers us a perspective from which we can connect to Thoreau's "natural day," gather strength and, notably, to see alternatives.

In a slower paced world, we will have less need for excessive material wealth and will not fall victim as often to the race for bigger and better. As one small example, there will be less pressure to move into ever bigger homes that exceed our needs, sap our time and strength and require huge amounts of energy to heat and cool. It will be possible for our lives to be powered without the vast amount of fossil fuel and nuclear energy that we need now, and to move towards renewable energy sources.

In a slower paced world, we will have time for the challenges and questions that face us. We will have time to contemplate and appreciate our homes, our food, our transportation, our families, our friends; all in relationship to our place. We will envision and realize ways of living that are beautiful, elegant, and functional and yet do not rest on the premise of unrelenting growth. And, we will come to know these things not as hopelessly utopian musings, but as solid, ageless wisdom.

Both the circular and linear perspectives of time have been useful to people and neither should be discarded as entirely unreasonable or unworkable. However, neither is practical by itself anymore. Because our awareness and knowledge of the world has changed so much, it may be impossible to return to a purely circular view of time. But a strictly linear view is not very satisfying and leads us to collective breakdown.

If both the circular and linear ways of imagining time are not serving us well, perhaps we can combine the two and create a new story – a story of *spiral time*. This would allow us to celebrate and rejoin the rhythms of the rest of Nature much more than we do now, and still to acknowledge our Human nature. With a concept of spiral time, we could justify our Human tendency to want to accumulate and plan for the future, but only to a point. With stories based on spiral time to guide us, the point at which our condition begins to worsen, rather than improve, will be more easily recognized. We will be able to temper our desires, to draw back and rest. We can find more satisfaction by measuring our progress in terms of those things that speak *directly* to our quality of life instead of indirectly (such as when we use secondary measures such as the production of goods and services). A less extractive and wasteful economy would be the natural result of these outlooks and actions, thus alleviating the pressure put the living systems of Earth that sustain us.

A spiral notion of time blends the arrow of our modern existence with the wisdom of the circle, yielding a new understanding of Nature and our place in it. Metaphorically, we can understand the creative forces of Life as the spiral DNA molecule and the destructive forces as a spiraling tornado. Just as Life gives way to death and springs again from it, the spirals double back on themselves in a grand cyclical dance.

Next to time, the way we consider, use and share energy is perhaps the most important element of any new vision for the future. In fact, there is a strong relationship between energy and time. The simple invention of the light bulb, and the electrical power grid that followed soon thereafter, offer an example. Until electrical lights extended the day with their glow, people's lives were slower by necessity. "Early to bed and early to rise," was the norm and the period of sleep varied with the seasons. Candles and even gaslights were of no consequence when compared to the surge of electrical energy and light that swept across the country starting in the early 1900's. Suddenly, we created an extended day in which to do more.

Light bulbs were the harbinger of much more to come. The rapid development of new technologies ranging from cars and airplanes to computers and washing machines allowed us to do more in less time. All of these required increasing amounts and reliability of energy. As with so many trends in modern life, we reached and passed a point of diminishing returns. The net effect of our constant growth has been the sapping of Human energy and the tapping of fossil energy around the globe. A vision of the future must include an understanding of Human nature with respect to both time and energy.

New insights from James Lovelock and Lynn Margulis into how Nature works offer a robust analogy for how Human systems – especially energy systems – can be best developed. Somewhat myopic views of Darwinian evolution have been used to guide and justify Human activity for more than a century. For instance, "Social Darwinism," a school of thought that explained Human social order almost exclusively through the lens of competition, arose in Europe in the late 1800s. Phrases such as "survival of the fittest" and "Nature red in tooth and claw" (the latter, from an earlier poem by Lord Tennyson and never used by Darwin) were used by both critics and supporters of Social Darwinism. But the biggest challenge for Humanity in the 21st century will be to add the lens of cooperation: to intentionally find and design ways of Life that mirror the *unconscious cooperation* among different kinds of microorganisms two to three billions of years ago. Just as new associations were essential for the continuation of Life in general eons ago, cooperative associations may be essential for the continuation of Human life in modern times.

Human society is at the same kind of crossroads now that Life was in its primacy. We rely on stored, high-energy molecules – fossil fuel – for almost everything we do, and in ever increasing amounts. Just as ancient bacteria solved their problem by harnessing the Sun's daily incoming energy and establishing partnerships between large and small systems, *our society has the opportunity to do exactly the same thing.* We can develop renewable energy resources such as solar and wind, like Japan and some European countries are already doing at levels much higher than we are in the US. Large systems (companies, governments and others) can form partnerships with medium and small systems rather than colonizing, dismantling or annihilating them. These can be truly symbiotic relationships that are advantageous to all involved and also in long-term balance with the rest of Life.

The insights afforded through the lens of Gaia Theory will provide much guidance as we seek to find our place in Nature and live in accord with it. Consider some of the opinions and thoughts of some of our world's most influential thinkers.

On July 4, 1994, Vaclav Havel (then the president of the Czech Republic) received the Philadephia Liberty Medal. In his acceptance speech at Independence Hall in Philadelphia, Havel pointed to the Gaia Hypothesis (and also the "Anthropic Principle - the idea that Human Beings are deeply and intricately connected to the entire Universe) as reasons for optimism for the future. He said that these two ideas "both remind us of what we have long suspected, of what we have long projected into our forgotten myths and what perhaps has always lain dormant within us as archetypes. That is, the awareness of our being anchored in the Earth and the Universe, the awareness that we are not here alone nor for ourselves alone but that we are an integral part of higher, mysterious entities . . ."[11]

Freeman Dyson, one of the world's foremost physicists, and once one of the most tireless champions of space exploration, came to a very similar conclusion.

> *One hopeful sign of sanity in modern society is the popularity of the idea of Gaia, invented by James Lovelock to personify our living planet. Respect for Gaia is the beginning of wisdom . . . As humanity moves into the future and takes control of its evolution, our first priority must be to preserve our emotional bond to Gaia. This bond must be our pulley. If it stays intact, then our species will remain fundamentally sane. If Gaia survives, then human complexity will survive too.12*

Many others have commented on the practical value of Gaia Theory. Just as the theory of evolution spawned new practices and improvements in medicine and agriculture, Gaia Theory can be the foundation for the design of human systems for energy, wastewater treatment, agriculture and everything else we do. Ultimately, our Human economy must fit in with the realities of Earth's living system for it to be sustainable. As increasing numbers of people consider the implications of Gaia Theory they will be able to see how it measures up in an epistemological manner – against ancient and traditional thought, modern scientific inquiry, common sense, empirical observations, and other ways of knowing. All of these will be most easily assessed within the context of particular places on Earth.

One of the most fascinating interdisciplinary links to be made through this new view of Life on Earth is the true place of Human society in the immensely old Gaian system. No longer can Human behavior and mannerisms, cultures, or even religions be considered entities separate from Nature as a whole. We begin to see how the stories, clothes, foods, and even thought patterns of different cultures are marvelous adaptations of Human Beings to the places in which we have evolved. With this viewpoint, we can rise to the challenge of creating *new* cultural adaptations that flow from our place and allow us to live in better balance with the rest of Nature.

The creation of a new story to better serve our needs cannot happen by edict or committee but will evolve as many people thoughtfully consider our place in Nature and come to new realizations. With my own observations as prelude, I arrive at a vision of my place at some time in the future . . . Fifteen years? Twenty? Forty? It is hard to say. As many look, metaphorically, to the East this vision will blend with theirs and grow into new ways of Life.

A Vision

Now, I gaze across to the East post of the circle garden. I close my eyes and let a dream grow through the "Eye of the Hawk." This is what I see.

I see people getting to know the land that they live in and spend most of their time. They celebrate the blooming of the bloodroot in the Spring and the blood reds of maple leaves in the Fall. As they behold Sunlight reflecting off tiny crystals of mica in the soil they contemplate their land's ancient story. I see people spending more time with their families and their neighbors. In this new day, they see themselves and others as *reflections* of the land itself. This may seem strange to the average American at the dawning of the 21st century, but, in my vision, people do see themselves as part of the land. They intimately understand that the physical matter of their bodies flows from and returns to the land, air and water. In the features of their place, they see stories of people, past and present. They see themselves as one glorious form of Life, among many, and celebrate and flourish in this realization.

I see people spending much of their time walking, picnicking and on forays into this hundred-acre-wood and its surrounding communities. Outings often include people of all ages; teenagers and young adults along with children and older adults. The elderly are active where they can be, more sedentary where necessary, but a big part of the community. They are called upon to share their life experiences and observations. I see men and women who fully acknowledge their desires and drives, but who also respect the value of limits.

I see a circle garden. Perhaps it is inspired by the circle garden that exists in the present day hundred-acre forest, or perhaps it is drawn from other traditions. It is hard to say, for the basic, universal truth of the circle and four directions is widely appreciated and there are many such sanctuaries around town. Large, small, simple or ornate; all of these gardens are places for personal reflection or group rituals that link people and place. They help people blend disparate parts of their lives and see them in the context of their community and land. This communion provides people with meaning and contentment that the unrelentingly pace and fury of the past had diluted and confused. No longer is Life seen as evolving simply in one direction of supposed material *progress*, but rather as a dance of opposites. The crisp, long shadows of bare branches brush over the garden in Winter, marking time in balance with the resplendent monarch butterflies that visit in late Summer. People recognize counterparts in the Human soul.

In my vision, I see a celebration at the shores of the Potomac River. People are swimming at the Donaldsons' Swimming Landing again. People of all ages and backgrounds are here, fishing, swimming, sailing and soaking in the beauty, power and sustenance of the river. They came on foot and made a day of it. The sand left by the last, raging flood on the Potomac is soft underfoot. A child is sitting atop a rock near the shore, staring down into an eddy of water in which a damselfly swirls atop raft of pondweed.

Can you feel the time scale of this day? The celebration – just one of many such scenes around town – is not one of idleness, but reflects the very essence of Life. It is a "natural day" in which time allows friends, family and place soak into our being without the multitudinous cares and details that flood life at the dawn of the 21st century! If all of our riches and technology cannot provide us with just this, of what value are they? We need time to learn the currents of the river and the wind and to sense the subtle arrival of Fall or Spring. If modern life removes us from understanding these basic elements of our place, what has it really afforded us?

In my vision, peoples' work blends with everyday life much more seamlessly than in the present day. The economy of this community is more secure and stable than in the day when essentially every material and all energy used in a place were from somewhere else. People are more content in their work, not restlessly seeking the next higher-paying position as often nor being forced to move on. The slower pace does not detract from the economic wellbeing of people but enriches it. For instance, the fishermen along the Potomac are not taking away from the success of the grocer by catching their own food, for the grocer, too, is on the river that day. The grocer is freed incrementally from having to sell a few extra fish by the fact that she gained things of value that did not cost money. On this day, there is a bounty of shad and striped bass for the fishermen; for the grocer, there is glorious, luxuriant time to spend with her family in the heaven and haven of this place. People in this vision have not transcended the use of money but simply recognize and live by the understanding that money cannot buy many of the most basic and important things in Life.

I see another celebration now, a late-Summer dinner in someone's yard with dozens of people at long tables, sitting in the glow of torches, eating a feast prepared from this land. The eggplant came from the garden yards away while tomatoes, potatoes, corn, green beans, and blackberries were brought from other household gardens. Even apartment dwellers tend to have container gardens on their balconies, and many buildings have rooftop gardens and "edible landscaping." One of those fishermen has brought a large catch of catfish and bass, now the prize entrée at the dinner. People are telling stories. The night is passing; no one is rushed. With youthful enthusiasm, a ninety-year-old man is relating the remarkable transformations of Arlington during his lifetime. Some of the youngest can't believe such worlds ever existed; some of the elders can't believe life is as it is now.

This is not Utopian folly. This kind of gathering is not the constant occupation of the people in my vision, simply more common and more desired than it is today. People yearn for this communion and are not distracted from attaining it by excess clutter. In this vision, most of the food for everyday life is still grown on farms – albeit much closer than in the present day – but almost everyone has relearned much of what their not-too-distant ancestors knew about growing, catching, preserving and preparing their own sustenance. They enjoy it and take a measure of confidence in it. There is a greater sense and appreciation of place and the fact that people's lives flow from Life as a whole.

A subtle part of the vision now enters my thoughts. The clothes, furniture, houses and other belongings around me are of fine quality. They are very durable and attractive, some in the aged manner of antiques so valued today. People know the stories of these items. In many cases, they were handmade at home or by friends or others in the community. A small, community-based textile industry grew out of a weaving program for mentally handicapped citizens. Much of the fiber is actually grown locally, and the beauty of the cloth is enhanced by the stories woven in with these fibers. Those few possessions acquired from faraway places are prized possessions, because people take care to discover the origins of these treasures as well.

Storerooms, closets and landfills are not filled with seldom or never-used things. A new materialism, in which people understand and appreciate the kinds and origins of materials used in everyday life, has replaced the old materialism characterized by massive rates of purchase and disposal of "stuff" of unknown origin. People generally use less of everything than they do today, but they do not feel needy in large part because they are not bombarded with messages that say they *should* feel that way. To the contrary, the new cultural norms balance acquisition with a strong sense of what is enough. For children growing up in this time, the concept of "conspicuous consumption" of previous generations is hard to understand. They find odd, and even a bit barbaric, the great lengths to which people went to increase material acquisition even when it detracted from their lives or was at the expense of the Living System upon which they depended.

In my vision I see children with smiles on their faces and confidence in their hearts. They are more involved in daily life and practical maintenance of families and communities than children of the present day; they are valued and much is expected of them. However, there is far more childhood freedom than was afforded to children in the past whose time was so tremendously structured. Children explore and play, and learn their place with timeless abandon. They soak it in like the air they breathe. They learn how to fish and garden, how to tell stories and how to spend time alone. They learn the concept of what is enough, and seldom feel hurried. Issues of self-esteem, so much the concern of the present day, have melted away like snow in the Sun.

In this vision, I see second graders helping to tend gardens at home and school. They eat what they grow and know the necessity of providing their plants good care. In another season, I see fifth graders with long-handled squeegees clearing snow off of solar panels. They are off to go sledding soon, but this is a duty expected of them and they do it with pride and playfulness. Last Fall, a group of high school students hired themselves out to winterize sunrooms that are now a standard part of the South side of most houses. (This and a host of other simple and wise features have made new homes and public buildings energy self-sufficient.) Springtime brings a new flurry of activity as the windows come off and the screens go up. There are dozens of relatively simple jobs like this one that teens fill admirably in this new world. As they participate in them, they learn directly the systems that keep the largely solar-powered infrastructure of their community operating smoothly.

Children and youth are never long away from the company and guidance of the oldest people of the community. They mentor youth or take them on as apprentices, imparting their knowledge, skills and stories. I see a white-haired man leading a class of school kids on a fieldtrip through the neighborhood. He is telling stories about some of the houses and former occupants. An old woman is teaching art – the passion of her life – to a high school class. She is well-known for her skill and use of vivid colors, but also her style that blurs the lines between her Human subjects and the plants, animals, river and the Sun shining down on her place. Her students are beginning to learn her skills and her insights. A group of retired engineers coaches the high school science club and just recently mentored a group of college students who retrofitted a wing of the high school with a passive solar energy and lighting features, insulation and a solar array on the roof. These senior citizens help guide the activities of the community and add gentle direction when disagreements arise. Elders are not peripheral; they are respected, valued and enmeshed with the community.

My vision is replete with families. Although each generation – children, youth, adults and old folks – are confidently autonomous in many ways, that strength comes from their families and from their place. Families have their feet on the Earth and their minds are kept in accord with each other through this attachment. There is affection and hope for each and every child. These are solid people I see. They are confident in their own abilities and those of people around them; not fearful of what the future might bring.

One of the most common and cherished family activities is learning about the world around them. They learn about and get to know every tree, geological feature and stream in their neighborhood. They delight in hearing the newly arrived Wood Thrush and other migrant birds, and in the stately progression of wildflowers from season to season. The wisdom of honoring and holding true to the changing seasons of this place makes sense to them and shows itself through an annual cycle of activities, activity levels, rituals, and diet. More than just enjoying the esthetics of their place, people have learned to work *with* the rest of Nature, rather than against it, in almost everything they do. Hot, steamy Summer days are once again a time for slowing down, and sitting in the shade. Perhaps even for contemplating connections.

In my vision there is still strife and friction, jealousy, abuse and divorce, but most families temper these emotions and problems with mutual support. The phrase "keeping up with the Joneses" is yet a part of the lexicon, but it has taken on an adolescent ring. Temptations and self-image are tempered with responsibility and self-knowledge. Tempered, but not replaced. The drive to acquire and be recognized are truly Human and could (and should) not be eradicated. In my vision, people recognize that these traits have their place, but in proper measure.

I see a house raising! A hundred people. Hammers ringing, saws flashing, the grunts of Human exertion. Children run back and forth with tools, hardware and drinks. Men and women are working alongside teenagers as the house goes up. A fallen white oak and a felled pine, milled nearby, provide much of the structure and flooring. A friend has turned out some handsome cabinets and furniture with some of the oak as well. The family is already telling stories about that tree that will be handed down to the grandkids. The house and the furniture will last longer. A rock foundation reclaimed from an old structure nearby will see to that; the slabs of granite gneiss have the same integrity as the day they were quarried. The skill and hard work are a thing of beauty. Food – lots of it – fills tables that everyone gathers around at the end of the day.

As much as this vision of the future is not like today, it is certainly not one of regression to old ways either. Life has evolved in a spiral manner. Its slower overall pace does not equate with boredom or backwardness, but with a more Human-scale rhythm. People are comfortable with new technologies and systems, but do not promote them for their own sake or as tools for an ever-expanding economy.

Businesses often close at lunch and people take leisure time much more readily than in the modern day. There are as many kinds of amusements and diversions as in the present day, but most require very little energy or material, substituting for them creativity instead. People have come to realize that modern productivity can be harnessed to allow more time for activities that are fun, interesting and nourishing – not just to produce more and more. Value is attached to the "free" offerings of

Life that people in the past could not enjoy simply because they required the time they did not have.

In this vision, I see that all manner of competitive activities. Races, games, musical contests. There are still a number of sports familiar to the old-timers. Football is still a passion. Wrestling matches are popular. Competition plays an important role in business and other aspects of everyday life as well. People have not let the pendulum swing so far as to lose sight of the essential competitive side of Life; they simply see it as firmly imbedded in the *cooperative* ties that bind all parts of their world together. These insights are not accidental or transient but are, instead, much-discussed tenets of society stemming from scientific understandings and the contemplation of place. Even more than great discoveries of the past – ranging from evolution to the genetic code – the new understanding of Life as a Gaian system guides and enriches people's lives.

People still take pride in being the best at whatever they do. They feel self-conscious when they do not measure up as well as they would like in terms of their dress, possessions and abilities. However, the emphasis on such matters is much relaxed compared to today's standards. Far from resulting in a lowest common denominator – as was feared – the paradigm in my vision is that of excellence of a sort yearned for by people in the present day. The craftsmanship, musical genius, and other abilities of an older world have rejoined the cutting edge of new ideas.

Cabinetmakers, artists, farmers and storytellers are once again integral parts of the community. Engineers, business people, doctors and religious leaders rub elbows with them at all turns, for all have come to see the need to understand each others' skills and points of view. And all people rub elbows with Life around them. People know their place; it is part of their very being.

In my vision, I see that people's jobs are almost all infused with variety. Most entail the use of head, heart *and* muscle to some measure.

Physical labor is a part of almost everyone's work, but hardly anyone minds. To the contrary, getting outside, moving about and even exerting one's body are all now seen as normal and expected parts of daily work. Those who remember the ways things were done before, shudder at the memory of spending all day in an office cubicle or cashier line. They are thankful for the dissolution of the curious social stigma that people in the past attached to physical labor. People are by all measures happier and healthier as a result.

In this future day, there are greater numbers of small to medium-sized businesses and fewer large ones than in present times. And, where large businesses exist, they form symbiotic partnerships with smaller businesses and communities. Systems of checks and balances observed in Nature have been incorporated into these relationships. Everything from entertainment to energy, from building materials to food production, is more localized than a generation ago, and communities have much more direct control over their own destinies. The local solar energy and architecture company, located in Georgetown, is a big employer with 500 employees, and it helps provide energy needs for most in the region. Houses are being built facing South again, and all have solar water heaters and passive architectural features to minimize heating and cooling needs. Solar electric panels, manufactured less than 50 miles away and on most rooftops, provide most of the electrical needs for buildings.

One of the best known businesses is the playhouse in nearby Clarendon. The cast is largely made up of graduates of Washington-Lee, a high school with a long tradition of producing excellent actors. The clothing manufacturer up on Lee Highway employs 250 people and is well know as being the first such business to switch entirely to non-synthetic materials, all grown within 300 miles. Old garments can actually be traded in for discounts on new clothes because they are sold by the manufacturer to a company that gleans compostables from various sources and sells the finished product to farmers. A shift in land-use has occurred during the last generation to allow some small farms to reappear, a few within five miles! These and other businesses thrive and flourish, providing people with goods and services they need as well as challenging, creative work.

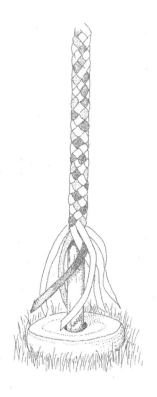

A final scene of this vision takes place on a warm, May evening in a grassy field in the middle of the woods. A few hours earlier, the field had been full of people and activity but it is now quiet. Just off the side of the road, a Maypole and its multicolored strands stand as testimony to some of that earlier activity. Below the snugly woven pattern sheathing the pole, the lower ends of the strands ruffle softly in the breeze. Each child had danced around the pole spiraling in and out and crossing their strand over and under those that other children were carrying. They all danced to the same music around the same pole, and at the end of the song were greeted by enthusiastic applause from parents and other onlookers.

This ritual has been performed by third-graders each Spring for more years than people can remember and there are families in which 3 generations have participated. Everyone looks forward to the dance, not just as a rite of the season, but as a metaphor for Human lives enmeshed with all of Nature. The strands were woven and gathered at the center of the dance as our collective lives gather around the places we live. The Maypole conjures up images of the earlier scene, and reminds me that as beautiful as the woven strands might be, the enduring beauty is that of the dance itself. The memory of it wafts in the evening breezes. I see a couple sitting on a bench at the edge of the field. A family walks by, laughing and happy. No one is in a hurry. There is time enough to attend to other demands and activities.

Can you see it with me? My vision can only capture a tiny sliver of what Life might be like in a time that celebrates and is informed by place. Life is rich with not only the world of Human construct, but also with a tapestry of rediscovered relationships with the rocks, air, water, sunlight, animals, plants, microbes, fungi and mysteries of Earth. To foresee that day in its entirety will take all of us, each creating a part of the vision. Perhaps you will write the next chapter.

CONCLUSION

As Europeans arrived in this area along the Potomac River 400 years ago, native cultures were massively disrupted by disease and conflict. Only hints of the stories that these native peoples lived by still exist. Just as a forest cleared of trees regenerates itself, however, a Human culture that is reflective of this place can also grow anew. The broad, archetypal motif of the circle and four directions, such as reflected in the Native American medicine wheel story, provides clues and direction for this cultural rebirth. It helps us fully develop our sense of place and urges us to pay attention to all aspects of our Nature – the ones that come easily to us and the ones that are harder.

In the opening pages of his book, *Seven Arrows*, Hycmeyohtsts Storm introduces themes and characters with which he lays out visions of the future. One of these characters is "a person called Hawk. The Hawk is the Little Brother of the Eagle. This person's Medicine Sign means that he was born with the gift of Seeing both at a Distance and Closely. Of course, this should be interpreted symbolically rather than literally . . . Hawk perceives with the illumination of the Golden East."[13] Hyemeyohtsts' story, like many others inspired by the circle and four directions, point us in the right direction. In the eye of the hawk, we can see our own vision.

"We shall not cease from exploration, and the end of all
our exploring shall be to arrive where we started
and know the place for the first time."
– T .S. Eliot

BIBLIOGRAPHY

1 McLain, Gary. 1990. The Indian Way; Learning to Communicate With Mother Earth. John Muir Publications, Santa Fe, New Mexico.

2 Italicized sections of "The Donaldsons" are adapted from the Human history section of the Potomac Overlook Regional Park Field Guide. Sections of the field guide were originally written by Martin Ogle, other park staff and volunteers. Dorothea Abbott was funded through a grant to help research the human history of the park, and contributed to the writing of these sections as well.

3 Neal, William. Georgia's Stone Mountain. (Booklet about Stone Mountain sold at the park. Undated, but with references as late as the 1970's)

4 Italicized sections of "Native Voices" are adapted from the Human history section of the Potomac Overlook Regional Park Field Guide. Sections of the field guide were originally written by Martin Ogle, other park staff and volunteers. Dorothea Abbott was funded through a grant to help research the human history of the park, and contributed to the writing of these sections as well.

5 This admonition against making a fool of any animal comes from a story I heard once about an Alaskan Indian's description of wolf-hunting from a helicopter.

6 Blanchan, Neltje. 1900. Nature's Garden: An Aid to Knowledge of Our Wildflowers and Their Insect Visitors. Doubleday, Page and Company, Garden City, NY.

7 Rifkin, Jeremy. 1989. Time Wars: The Primary Conflict in Human History. Simon and Schuster, New York

8 Thoreau, Henry David. 1854. Walden.

9   Darwin, Charles. 1876. My Several Publications. <u>In</u> Charles Darwin Autobiographies. 2002. Edited by Michael Neve and Sharon Messenger. Penguin Books, London, England. pp. 84-85.

10 Margulis, Lynn. 1998. Symbiotic Planet. Basic Books, New York

11 Havel, Vaclav. 1994. The Miracle of Being: Our Mysterious Interdependence. Acceptance speech for the Liberty Medal presented at Independence Hall, Philadephia, Pennsylvania, on July 4, 1994.

12 Dyson, Freeman. 1988. From Eros to Gaia. New York: Pantheon Books.

13 Storm, Hyemeyohsts. 1972. Seven Arrows. Ballantine Books, New York.

Made in the USA
Lexington, KY
15 September 2012